MEN, WOMEN, AND GODS
AND OTHER LECTURES

MEN, WOMEN, AND GODS

AND OTHER LECTURES

by Helen H. Gardner

Laurence E. Dalton and Shirley Strutton Dalton, Ed

To order additional copies of this book, contact:
Xlibris Corporation
1-888-7-XLIBRIS
www.Xlibris.com
Orders@Xlibris.com

CONTENTS

Introduction 9
Introduction by Robert G. Ingersoll 13
Men, Women, and Gods 18
Vicarious Atonement 60
Historical Facts And Theological Fictions 88
Address to the Clergy and Others 139
Letter to the Cleveland Congress of Freethinkers,
October 1885 142
Appendices 145

THIS LITTLE VOLUME

is

RESPECTFULLY DEDICATED,
WITH THE LOVE OF THE AUTHOR,
To
MRS. EVA INGERSOLL,
The brave, happy wife of America's greatest orator, and a
woman's truest friend. In her beautiful home-life superstition
and fear have never entered; human equality and freedom have
their highest illustration; and time has deepened youthful love
into a diviner worship than angels offer or than gods inspire.

INTRODUCTION

After a long and difficult struggle, women in the United States finally achieved the right to vote in federal elections in 1920. They not only claimed the right to vote, but claimed all rights as citizens and as persons. They claimed the right to control their lives, their children, their property, their earnings, their bodies, their minds. The vote was a step on the road to equal treatment, to liberty. The women who led the struggle, as well as those who worked in the trenches, and the men who helped them, believed they could overcome the oppression that had held women in chains for far too long.

Many women today, especially young women, believe that suffrage is a dead issue; it has been eighty years since that battle was won. Other battles have been fought and won; women own property, own businesses, work and control their own earnings, get divorces and are able to keep custody of their children. They have a right to reproductive control; a battle won in part because Margaret Sanger and others were willing to go to prison for that right. Some might even say the struggle is over; equality has been achieved. But has it?

The documents created by suffragists and antisuffragists in their struggle illuminate the cultural and intellectual values that shaped the 19th century and the decades that followed. It is time to remember the women who led the way and hear their voices. We can learn what they meant by home, marriage, and family and how these values determined their lives. Some of the same forces are still at work today to keep women from being treated as full persons. To Helen H. Gardener, one of the major forces oppressing women was religion, "Women have for a long time been asking for the right to an education, for the right to live on an equal footing with their brothers, and for the right to earn money honestly; while at the same time they have supported a book and a religion which hold them as the inferiors of their sons and as objects of contempt   and degradation . . . ." (H.H. Gardener, *Men, Women, and Gods*).

Helen Hamilton Gardener was born Mary Alice Chenoweth on January 21, 1853, in Winchester, Virginia, daughter of Katherine A. Peel and Rev. Alfred Griffith Chenoweth. She moved with her parents to Washington, D.C., and then to Indiana. In Washington, her father manumitted the slaves he had inherited and gave them the last of his savings to get them started in a new life before he moved with his family to Indiana.

Alice Chenoweth graduated from a Cincinnati (Ohio) high school and from the Ohio State Normal School for teachers in 1873. She married Charles S. Smart, a forty-year-old state school commissioner in Ohio, in 1875 and moved with him to New York City in 1880 where they lived until his death in 1901. She studied biology at Columbia University, lectured on sociology at the Brooklyn Institute of Arts and Sciences, and wrote magazine articles and short stories during that time. Many of these were later collected and published (see her books below).

Gardener became a protégé of the famous freethinker Colonel Robert G., and his wife Eva Ingersoll. He encouraged her to give a series of lectures on freethinking in 1884. These lectures were later published in 1885 as *Men, Women, and Gods, and Other Lectures* under the name Helen Hamilton Gardener, a name she subsequently adopted in her personal life. During this time, Gardener became friends with Elizabeth Cady Stanton and joined the revision committee for Stanton's *The Woman's Bible*. She was active in the woman's suffrage movement and highly instrumental in persuading President Woodrow Wilson to support the 19th Amendment.

She pursued her interest in biology, undertaking a study to disprove the common claim that women were inferior to men because they had smaller brains. Her findings, that there was no justification for this assertion, were presented in a paper, "Sex in Brain," to the Woman's International Congress held in Washington in 1888. The paper was later published in several medical journals and translated into eight languages. It became a standard work on the subject. After Gardener's husband died, she married Selden Allen Day in 1902, a colonel in the US Army. Upon his retirement, they spent six years traveling the world before settling in Washington, D.C. "She was invited to lecture at many of the universities in Japan, France, England, and Italy. She visited twenty countries making a comparative study of 'Ourselves and Other Peoples,' collecting pictures and data, and upon returning to the United States gave illustrated university extension lectures under the title quoted.

"She was decorated by the governments of France and Japan for her public work. She held the Peace Medal of France for her book *An Unofficial Patriot*, which Baron de Estronelles de Constant, of the Hague, said was a book that 'went all the way to peace,' and of which Senator John Sharp William said 'it contained the best verbal portrait of Abraham Lincoln to be found in our literature.'" [Votes for Women: Selections from the NAWSA Collection, 1848-1921, Library of Congress.]

In 1913 Gardener was appointed to reorganize the Congressional Committee of the National American Woman Suffrage Association [NAWSA], which had been depleted by mass resignations of radical suffragists and followers of Alice Paul. She was elected a vice president of the association in 1917. Her contacts, notably with President Wilson and Speaker of the House Champ Clark, along with her wit and tact, made her a central figure in the practical business of maneuvering the federal suffrage amendment through a maze of obstacles. In 1920 (following the ratification of the 19th Amendment granting women the right to vote) she was appointed by President Wilson to the U.S. Civil Service Commission, the highest federal position occupied by a woman to that time. She was held in high esteem and respect by her fellow commissioners and worked for enlightened personnel policies, fighting for justice and the rights of all persons, women and men. She served under three presidents (Wilson, Harding and Coolidge) until her death in Washington, D.C. on July 26, 1925, and was buried in Arlington National Cemetery beside her husband, Col. Day, who had died in 1918.

To present her ideas to the public, Gardener wrote two novels and several short stories. Her books include: *Is This Your Son, My Lord?* (1890); *A Thoughtless Yes* (1890), *Pray You, Sir, Whose Daughter?* (1892), *Pushed By Unseen Hands* (1892), and *An Unofficial Patriot* (1894), a fictionalized biography of her father that was later successfully dramatized by James A. Herne as *Griffith Davenport, Circuit Rider.* Many of her articles on social questions were collected in *Facts and Fictions of Life* (1893).

(Sources: Women's Studies Manuscript Collections from the Schlesinger Library, Radcliffe College, Introduction, www.cispubs.com/; Votes for Women: Selections from the NAWSA Collection, 1848-1921, Library of Congress; 1999 Encyclopædia Britannica, Inc.)

INTRODUCTION
BY ROBERT G. INGERSOLL

Nothing gives me more pleasure, nothing gives greater promise for the future, than the fact that woman is achieving intellectual and physical liberty. It is refreshing to know that here, in our country, there are thousands of women who think and express their own thoughts—who are thoroughly free and thoroughly conscientious—who have neither been narrowed nor corrupted by a heartless creed—who do not worship a being in heaven whom they would shudderingly loathe on earth. Women who do not stand before the altar of a cruel faith with downcast eyes of timid acquiescence, and pay to impudent authority the tribute of a thoughtless yes. They are no longer satisfied with being told. They examine for themselves. They have ceased to be the prisoners of society—the satisfied serfs of husbands or the echoes of priests. They demand the rights that naturally belong to intelligent human beings. If wives, they wish to be the equals of husbands—if mothers, they wish to rear their children in the atmosphere of love, liberty and philosophy. They believe that woman can discharge all her duties without the aid of superstition, and preserve all that is true, pure and tender without sacrificing in the temple of absurdity the convictions of the soul.

Woman is not the intellectual inferior of man. She has lacked—not mind—but opportunity. In the long night of barbarism physical strength, and the cruelty to use it, were the badges of superiority. Muscle was more than mind. In the ignorant age of Faith the loving nature of woman was abused, her conscience was rendered morbid and diseased. It might almost be said that she was betrayed by her own virtues. At best, she secured, not opportunity, but flattery, the preface to degradation. She was deprived of liberty and without that nothing is worth the having. She was taught to obey without question, and to believe without thought. There were universities for men before the alphabet had been taught to woman. At the intellectual feast there were no places for wives and mothers. Even now they sit at the second table and eat the crusts and crumbs. The schools for women, at the present time, are just far enough behind those for men to fall heirs to the discarded. On the same principle, when a doctrine becomes too absurd for the pulpit, it is given to the Sunday School. The ages of muscle and miracle—of fists and faith—are passing away. Minerva occupies at last a higher niche than Hercules. Now, a word is stronger than a blow.

At last we see women who depend upon themselves—who stand self poised the shocks of this sad world without leaning for support against a church—who do not go to the literature of barbarism for consolation, nor use the falsehoods and mistakes of the past for the foundation of their hope—women brave enough and tender enough to meet and bear the facts and fortunes of this world.

The men who declare that woman is the intellectual inferior of man, do not, and cannot, by offering themselves in evidence, substantiate their declaration.

Yet, I must admit that there are thousands of wives who still have faith in the saving power of superstition—who still insist on attending church while husbands prefer the shores, the woods, or the fields. In this way families are divided. Parents grow apart, and unconsciously the pearl of greatest price is thrown away. The wife ceases to be the intellectual companion of the husband. She reads the "Christian Register" sermons in the Monday papers, and a little gossip about folks and fashions, while he studies the works of Darwin, Haeckel and Humboldt. Their sympathies become estranged. They are no longer mental friends. The husband smiles at the follies of the wife and she weeps for the supposed sins of the husband. Such wives should read this book. They should not be satisfied to remain forever in the cradle of thought, amused with the toys of superstition. The parasite of woman is the priest.

It must also be admitted that there are thousands of men who believe that superstition is good for women and children—who regard falsehood as the fortress of virtue, and feel indebted to ignorance for the purity of daughters and the fidelity of wives. These men think of priests as detectives in disguise, and regard God as a policeman who prevents elopements. Their opinions about religion are as correct as their estimate of woman.

The church furnishes but little food for the mind. People of intelligence are growing tired of the platitudes of the pulpit—the iterations of the itinerants. The average sermon is "as tedious as a twice-told tale vexing the ears of a drowsy man."

One Sunday a gentleman who is a great inventor called at my house. Only a few words had passed between us, when he arose, saying that he must go as it was time for church. Wondering that a man of his mental wealth could enjoy the intellectual poverty of the pulpit, I asked for an explanation, and he gave me the following: "You know that I am an inventor. Well, the moment my mind becomes absorbed in some difficult problem, I am afraid that something may happen to distract my attention. Now, I know that I can sit in church for an hour without the slightest danger of having the current of my thought disturbed."

Most women cling to the Bible because they have been taught that to give up that book is to give up all hope of another life—of ever meeting again the loved and lost. They have also been taught that the Bible is their friend, their defender, and the real civilizer of man.

Now if they will only read this book—these three lectures, without fear, and then read the Bible, they will see that the truth or falsity of the dogma of inspiration has nothing to do with the question of immortality. Certainly the Old Testament does not teach us that there is another life, and upon that question, even the New is obscure and vague. The hunger of the heart finds only a few small and scattered crumbs. There is nothing definite, solid, and satisfying. United with the idea of immortality we find the absurdity of the resurrection. A prophecy that depends for its fulfillment upon an impossibility, cannot satisfy the brain or heart.

There are but few who do not long for a dawn beyond the night. And this longing is born of, and nourished by, the heart. Love wrapped in shadow—bending with tear-filled eyes above its dead, convulsively clasps the outstretched hand of hope.

I had the pleasure of introducing Helen H. Gardener to her first audience, and in that introduction said a few words that I will repeat.

"We do not know, we can not say whether death is a wall or a door, the beginning or end of a day, the spreading of pinions to soar, or the folding forever of wings. The rise or the set of a sun, of an endless life that brings rapture and love to every one.

"Under the seven-hued arch of hope let the dead sleep."

They will also discover, as they read the "Sacred Volume," that it is not the friend of woman. They will find that the writers of that book, for the most part, speak of woman as a poor beast of burden—a serf, a drudge, a kind of necessary evil—as mere property. Surely a book that upholds polygamy is not the friend of wife and mother.

Even Christ did not place woman on an equality with man. He said not one word about the sacredness of home, the duties of the husband to the wife—nothing calculated to lighten the hearts of those who bear the saddest burdens of this life.

They will also find that the Bible has not civilized mankind. A book that establishes and defends slavery and wanton war is not calculated to soften the hearts of those who believe implicitly that it is the work of God. A book that not only permits, but commands religious persecution, has not in my judgment developed the affection nature of man. Its influence has been bad and bad only. It has filled the world with bitterness, revenge, and crime, and retarded in countless ways the progress of our race.

The writer of this little volume has read the Bible with open eyes. The mist of sentimentality has not clouded her vision. She has had the courage to tell the result of her investigations. She has been quick to discover contradictions. She appreciates the humorous side of the stupidly solemn. Her heart protests against the cruel, and her brain rejects the childish, the unnatural, and absurd. There is no misunderstanding between her head and heart. She says what she thinks, and feels what she says.

No human being can answer her arguments. There is no answer. All the priests in the world cannot explain away her objections. There is no explanation. They should remain dumb, unless they can show that the impossible is the probable—that slavery is better than freedom—that polygamy is the friend of woman—that the innocent can justly suffer for the guilty, and that to persecute for opinion's sake is an act of love and worship.

Wives who cease to learn—who simply forget and believe, will fill the evening of their lives with barren sighs and bitter tears. The mind should outlast youth.

If, when beauty fades, Thought, the deft and unseen sculptor, hath not left his subtle lines upon the face, then all is lost. No charm is left. The light is out. There is no flame within to glorify the wrinkled clay.

ROBERT G. INGERSOLL, Hoffman House, New York, July 22, 1885.

MEN, WOMEN, AND GODS

It is thought strange and particularly shocking by some persons for a woman to question the absolute correctness of the Bible. She is supposed to be able to go through the world with her eyes shut, and her mouth open wide enough to swallow Jonah and the Garden of Eden without making a wry face. It is usually recounted as one of her most beautiful traits of character that she has faith sufficient to float the Ark without inspecting the animals.

So it is thought strange that a woman should object to any of the teachings of the Patriarchs. I claim, however, that if she honestly thinks there is anything wrong about them she has a right to say so. I claim that I have a right to offer my objections to the Bible from the standpoint of a woman. I think that it is fair, at least, to put the case before you as it looks to me, using the Bible itself as my chief witness. That Book I think degrades and belittles women, and I claim the right to say why I think so. The opposite opinion has been stated by hundreds of people, hundreds of times, for hundreds of years, so that it is only fair that I be allowed to bring in a minority report.

Women have for a long time been asking for the right to an education, for the right to live on an equal footing with their brothers, and for the right to earn money honestly; while at the same time they have supported a book and a religion which hold them as the inferiors of their sons and as objects of contempt and degradation with Jehovah. They have sustained a so-called "revelation" which holds them as inferior and unclean things. Now it has always seemed to me that these women are trying to stand on both sides of the fence at the same time—and that neither foot touches.

I think they are making a mistake. I think they are making a mistake to sustain any religion which is based upon faith. Even though a religion claim a superhuman origin—and I believe they all claim that—it must be tested by human reason, and if our highest moral sentiments revolt at any of its dictates, its dictates must go. For the only good thing about any religion is its morality, and morality has nothing to do with faith. The one has to do with right actions in this world; the other with unknown quantities in the next. The one is a necessity of time the other a dream of Eternity. Morality depends upon universal evolution; Faith upon special "revelation"; and no woman can afford to accept any "revelation" that has yet been offered to this world.

That Moses or Confucius, Mohammed or Paul, Abraham or Brigham Young asserts that his particular dogma came directly from God, and that it was a personal communication to either or all of these favored individuals, is a fact that can have no power over us unless their teachings are in harmony with our highest thought, our noblest purpose, and our purist conception of life. Which of them can bear the test? Not one "revelation" known to man to-day can look in the face of the nineteenth century and say, "I am parallel with your richest development; I still lead your highest thought; none of my teachings shock your sense of justice." Not one.

It is faith in "revelation" that makes a mother tear from her arms a tender, helpless child and throw it in the Ganges—to appease the gods! It is a religion of faith that teaches the despicable principle of caste—and that religion was invented by those who profited by caste. It was our religion of faith that sustained the institution of slavery—and it had for its originators dealers in human flesh. It is the Mormon's religion of faith, his belief in the Bible and in the wisdom of Solomon and David, that enables the monster of polygamy to flaunt its power and its filth in the face of morality of the nineteenth century, which has outgrown the Jehovah of the Jews.

Every religion must be tried at the bar of human justice, and stand or fall by the verdict there. It has no right to crouch behind the theory of "inspiration" and demand immunity from criticism; and yet that is just what every one of them does. They all claim that we have no right to use our reason on their inventions. But evil cannot be made good by revelation, and good cannot be made evil by persecution.

A "revelation" that teaches us to trample on purity, or bids us despise beauty—that gives power to vice or crushes the weak—is an evil. The dogma that leads us to ignore our humanity, that asks us to throw away our pleasures, that tells us to be miserable here in order that we may be happy hereafter, is a doctrine built upon a false philosophy, cruel in its premises and false in its promises. And the religion that teaches us that believing Vice is holier than unbelieving Virtue is a grievous wrong. Credulity is not a substitute for morality. Belief is not a question of right or wrong, it is a question of mental organization. Man cannot believe what he will, he must believe what he must. If his brain tells him one thing and his catechism tells him another, his brain ought to win. You don't leave your umbrella at home during a storm, simply because the almanac calls for a clear day.

A religion that teaches a mother that she can be happy in heaven, with her children in hell—in everlasting torment—strikes at the very roots of family affection. It makes the human heart a stone. Love that means no more than that, is not love at all. No heart that has ever loved can see the object of its affection in pain and itself be happy. The thing is impossible. Any religion that can make that possible is more to be dreaded than war or famine or pestilence or death. It would eat out all that is great and beautiful and good in this life. It would make life a mockery and love a curse.

I once knew a case myself, where an oldest son who was an unbeliever died. He had been a kind son and a good man. He had shielded his widowed mother from every hardship. He had tried to lighten her pain and relieve her loneliness. He had worked early and late to keep her comfortable and happy. When he died she was heartbroken. It seemed to her more than she could bear. As she sat and gazed at his dear face in a transport of grief, the door opened and her preacher came in to bring her the comfort of religion. He talked with her of her loss, and finally he said, "But it would not be so hard for you to bear if he had been a Christian. If he had accepted what was freely offered him you would one day see him again. But he chose his path, he denied his Lord, and he is lost. And now, dear madam, place your affections on your living son, who is, thank God, saved." That was the comfort he brought her. That was the consolation of his religion. I am telling you of an actual occurrence. This is all a fact. Well, a few years later that dear old lady died in her son's house, where she had gone on a visit. He broke her will—this son who was saved—and brought in a bill against her estate for her board and nursing while she was ill! Which one of those boys do you think would be the best company for her in the next world?

It has always seemed to me that I would rather go to hell with a good son than to heaven with a good Christian. I may be wrong, but with my present light that is the way it looks to me; and for the sake of humanity I am glad that it looks that way.

A church member said to me some time ago that even though the Bible were not "the word of God," even though it were not necessary to believe in the creed in order to go to heaven, it could not do any harm to believe it; and he thought it was "best to be on the safe side, for," said he, "suppose after all it should happen to be true!" So he carries a church-membership as a sort of accident insurance policy.

I do not believe we have a right to work upon that basis. It is not honest. I do not believe that any "suppose it should be" gives us the right to teach "I know that it is." I do not believe in the honesty and right of any cause that has to prop up its backbone with faith, and splinter its legs with ignorance. I do not believe in the harmlessness of any teaching that is not based upon reason, justice, and truth. I do not believe that it is harmless to uphold any religion that is not noble and elevating in itself. I do not believe that it is "just as well" to spread any dogma that stultifies reason and ignores common-sense. I do not believe that it is ever well to compromise with dishonesty and pretence. And I cannot admit that it "can do no harm" to teach a belief in the goodness of a God who sends an Emerson or a Darwin to hell because Eve was fond of fruit, and who offers a reserved seat in heaven to Chastine Cox because a mob murdered Jesus Christ. It does not seem to me good morals, and it is certainly poor logic.

And speaking of logic, I heard a funny story the other day about one of those absurdly literal little girls who, when she heard people say they "wanted to be an angel," did not know it was a joke. She thought it was all honor-bright. She was standing by the window killing flies, and her mother called her and said, "Why child, don't you know that is very wicked? Don't you know that God made those dear little flies, and that he loves them?" (Just imagine an infinite God in love with a blue-bottle fly!) Well, the little girl thought that was queer taste, but she was sorry, and said that she would not do it any more. By and by, however, a great lazy fly was too tempting, and her plump little finger began to follow him around slowly on the glass, and she said, "Oh you nice big fly, did dod nade you? And does dod love you? And does you love dod?" (Down came the finger.) "Well, you shall see him."

Yet we all know Christians who love God better than anything else—"with all their hearts and soul and strength"—who prefer to postpone seeing him till the very last minute. They say it is because they have not "fulfilled their allotted time." Why not be honest and say it is because they like to live? They "long to put on immortality." But their sleep is sounder if they live next door to a good doctor.

People say that men are infidels because it is easier—to rid themselves of responsibility. But it seems to me that anyone who advances the doctrine of "morality and works" instead of that of "repentance and faith," on the ground that it is easier, is laboring under a mistake. I don't see how any one could ask for an easier way of getting rid of his sins than the plan that simply unloads them on to another man. I fail to see anything hard about that—

except for the man who catches the load; and I am unable to see anything commendable about it either. But it is not always easy for a man to be brave enough to be responsible for his own mistakes or faults. It is not always easy for a man to say "I did it, and I will suffer the penalty." That is not always easy, but it is always just. No one but a coward or a knave needs to shift his personal responsibility on to the shoulders of the dead. Honest men and women do not need to put "Providence" up between themselves and their own motives.

A short time ago the wife of a very devout man apparently died, but her body remained so lifelike and her color so natural that her relatives decided that she could not be dead, and they summoned a physician. The husband, however, refused to have him administer any restoratives. He said that if the Lord had permitted her to go into a trance and was anxious to bring her out alive he would do it. Meanwhile he did not intend to meddle with Providence. His maxim was, "Whatever else you do, don't interfere with Providence. Give Providence a good chance and if it doesn't come round all right for Betsy, I think I can bear it—and she will have to." If we take care of our motives toward each other, "Providence" will take care of itself.

Did you ever know a pious man do a real mean thing—that succeeded—who did not claim that Providence had a finger in it? The smaller the trick, the bigger the finger. He is perfectly honest in his belief too. He is the sort of man that never has a doubt about hell—and that most people go there. Thinks they all deserve it. Has entire confidence that God is responsible for every word in the Bible, and that all other Bibles and all other religions are the direct work of the devil. Probably prays for people who don't believe that way. He is perfectly honest in it. That is simply his size, and he usually pities anybody who wears a larger hat.

But they say this is not a matter of reason. This is outside of reason, it is all a matter of faith. But whenever a superstition claims to be so holy that you must not use your reason about it, there is something wrong some place. Truth is not afraid of reason, nor reason of truth.

I am going to say something to-night about why I do not believe in a religion of faith. I am going to tell you some of the reasons why I do not believe that the Bible is "inspired"; why I, as a woman, don't want to think it is the word of God; why I think that women, above all others, should not believe that it is. And since women are the bulwarks of the churches to-day, it seems to me they have the right, and that it is a part of their duty, to ask themselves why. Since about seven-tenths of all church-members are women, surely the churches should not deny them the right to use their reason (or whatever serves them in that capacity) in regard to their own work.

I saw some ladies begging the other day for money to pay off the debt of a $200,000 church, on the corner-stone of which were cut the words, "My kingdom is not of this world"; and I wondered at the time what the property would have been like if the kingdom had been of this world. It seemed to me that a few hundred such untaxed houses would be a pretty fair property almost anywhere.

One of our prominent bishops, when speaking recently of church-membership, said, "The Church must recruit her ranks hereafter almost entirely with children;" and he added, "the time has passed when she can recruit her ranks with grown men." Good! And the New York Evangelist (one of the strongest church papers) says, "Four-fifths of the earnest young men of this country are skeptics, distrust the clergy, and are disgusted with evangelical Christianity." Good again.

The Congregational Club of Boston has recently been discussing the question how to win young men to Christianity. The Rev. R.R. Meredith said: "The churches to-day do not get the best and sharpest young men. They get the goody-goody ones easily enough; but those who do the thinking are not brought into the church in great numbers. You cannot reach them by the Bible. How many did Moody touch in this city, during his revival days? You can count them on your fingers. The man who wants them cannot get them with the Bible under his arm. He must be like them, sharp. They cannot be gathered by sentimentality. If you say to them, 'Come to Jesus,' very likely they will reply; 'Go to thunder.' (In Boston!) The thing to be done with such a man is to first get into his heart, and then lead him into salvation before he knows it."

I don't know how good this recipe is, but I should infer that it is a double-back-action affair of some sort that could get into a man's heart and lead him into salvation before he knew it, and that if the Church can just get a patent on that she is all right; otherwise I suspect that the goody-goody ones are likely to be about all she will get in large numbers.

Do I need any stronger, plainer evidence than this to show that the thought of the world is against it, and that it is time for women to ask themselves whether a faith that can hold its own only by its grasp upon the ignorance and credulity of children, a faith that has made four-fifths of the earnest men skeptics, a faith that has this deplorable effect upon Boston manners, is one that does honor to the intellect and judgment of the women of to-day?

We hear women express indignation that the law classes them with idiots and children; but from these orthodox statements it would seem that in the Church they voluntarily accept about this classification themselves. If only these church-people go to heaven, what a queer kindergarten it will be, to be sure, with only a few male voices to join in the choruses—and most of those tenor.

This religion and the Bible require of woman everything, and give her nothing. They ask her support and her love, and repay her with contempt and oppression. No wonder that four-fifths of the earnest men are against it, for it is not manly and it is not just; and such men are willing to free women from the ecclesiastical bondage that makes her responsible for all the ills of life, for all the pains of deed and creed, while it allows her no choice in their formation, no property in their fruition. Such men are outgrowing the petty jealousies and musty superstitions of narrow-minded dogmatists sufficiently to look upon the question not as one of personal preference, but as one of human justice. They do not ask,

"Would I like to see woman do thus or thus?" but, "have I a right to dictate the limit of her efforts or her energy?"—not, "Am I benefitted by her ecclesiastical bondage and credulity? Does it give me unlimited power over her?" but, "Have I a right to keep in ignorance, have I a right to degrade, any human intellect?" And they have answered with equal dignity and impersonal judgment that it is the birthright of no human being to dominate or enslave another; that it is the just lot of no human being to be born subject to the arbitrary will or dictates of any living soul; and that it is, after all, as great an injustice to a man to make him a tyrant as it is to make him a slave.

Whenever a man rises high enough to leave his own personality out of the question, he has gone beyond the Stage of silly platitudes. His own dignity is too secure, his title to respect too far beyond question, for him to need such little subterfuges to guard his position, either as husband, as household-king, or as public benefactor. His home life is not founded upon compulsory obedience; but is filled with the perfume of perfect trust, the fragrance of loving admiration and respect. It is the domestic tyrant, the egotistic mediocre, and the superstitious Church that are afraid for women to think, that fear to lose her as worshipper and serf.

You need go only a very little way back in history to learn that the Church decided that a woman who learned the alphabet overstepped all bounds of propriety, and that She would be wholly lost to shame who should so far forget her modesty as to become acquainted with the multiplication table.

And to-day, if she offers her opinion and her logic for what they are worth, the clergy preach doleful sermons about her losing her beautiful home character, about her innocence being gone, about their idea of her glorious exaltation as wife and mother being destroyed. Then they grow florid and exclaim that "man is after all subject to her, that he is born for the rugged path and she for the couch of flowers!" (NOTE: "A pertinacious adversary, pushed to extremities, may say that husbands indeed are willing to be reasonable, and to make fair concessions to their partners without being compelled to it, but that wives are not; that if allowed any rights of their own they will acknowledge no rights at all in any one else, and never will yield in anything, unless they can be compelled, by the man's mere authority, to yield in everything. This would have been said by many persons some generations ago, when satires on women were in vogue, and men thought it a clever thing to insult women for being what men made them. But it will be said by no one now who is worth replying to. It is not the doctrine of the present day that women are less susceptible of good feeling and consideration for those with whom they are united by the strongest ties, than men are. On the contrary, we are perpetually told that women are better than men by those who are totally opposed to treating them as if they were as good; so that the saying has passed into a piece of tiresome cant, intended to put a complimentary face upon an injury."—John Stuart Mill.)

You recognize it all, I see. You seem to have heard it some-where before. I recall one occasion when I heard it from a country clergyman, who knew so much about heaven and hell that he hardly had time to know enough about this world to enable him to keep out of the fire unless he was tied to a chair. It was in the summer of 1876, and I remember the conversation began by his asking a lady in the room about the Centennial display, from which she had just returned. He asked her if she would advise him to take his daughter. She said she thought it would be a very nice thing for the girl, and she added, "It will be good for you. You will see so much that is new and wonderful. It will be of use to you in your work, I am sure." He said, "Well, I don't know about that. There won't be anything much that is new to me. I've seen it all. I was in Philadelphia in 1840." Then he gave us quite a talk on "woman's sphere." He could tell you in five minutes just what it was; and the amount of information that man possessed about the next world was simply astonishing. He knew pretty nearly everything. I think he could tell you, within a fraction or two, just how much mate-rial it took to make wings for John the Baptist, and whether Paul sings bass or tenor. His presbytery says he is a most remarkable theologian—and I don't doubt it. According to the law of compensation, however, what he does not know about this world would make a very comprehensive encyclopedia.

But seriously, did it ever occur to you to ask any of these divine oracles why, if all these recent compliments are true about the superior beauty and virtue and truth and power resting with women—why it is that they always desire as heirs sons rather than daughters? You would think their whole desire would be for girls, and that, like Oliver Twist, their chief regret would be that they hadn't "more." But the Bible (and the clergy, until quite recently) pronounces it twice as great a crime to be the mother of a girl as to be the mother of a boy. A crime to be the mother of a little child— a double crime if the child should be a girl.

It is often urged that women are better off under the Christian than under any other religion; that our Bible is more just to her than other Bibles are. For the time we will grant this, and respectfully inquire—what does it prove? If it proves anything it is this— that all "divine revelations" are an indignity to women, and that they had better stick to nature. Nature may be exacting, but she is not partial. If it proves anything, it is that all religions have been made by men for men and through men. I do not contend for the superiority of other Bibles, I simply protest against the wrong in ours. One wrong cannot excuse another. That murder is worse than arson does not make a hero of the rascal who fires our homes. If Allah were more cruel than Jehovah, that would be no palliation of the awful crimes of the Old Testament. That slaves have better clothes than savages cannot make noble traffic in human blood. A choice of evils is often necessary, but it does not make either of them a good. But there is no book which tells of a more infamous monster than the Old Testament, with its Jehovah of murder and cruelty and revenge, unless it be the New Testament, which arms its God with hell, and extends his outrages throughout all eternity!

Another argument is that if orthodox Christianity were not good for women they would not support and cling to it; if it did not comfort them they would discard it. In reply to that I need only recall to you the fact that it is the same in all religions. Women have ever been the stanchest [sic] defenders of the faith, the most bitter haters of an Infidel, the most certain that their form of faith is the only truth. Yet I do not hear this fact advanced to prove the divinity of the Koran or the book of Mormon. If it is a valid argument in the one case it is valid in the others. The trouble with it is it proves too much; it takes in the whole field. It does not leave a weed from the first incantation of the first aborigine to the last shout of the last convert to Mormonism, out of its range; and it does, and always has done, just as good service for any one of the other religions as it does for ours. It is a free-for-all, go-as-you-please argument; but it is the sort of chaff they feed theological students on—and they sift it over for women. It is pretty light diet when it gets to them—but it is filling.

Recently I heard a clergyman give the following as his reason for opposing medical, or scientific training of any sort, for women: "Now her whole energy and force of action (outside of the family) must be expended upon religion. If she were allowed other fields of action or thought, her energy, like that of man, would be withdrawn from and fatally cripple the Church."

To me, however, it seems that any organization that finds it necessary to cripple its adherents in order to keep them has a screw loose somewhere.

And it also seems to me that it is time for women to try to find out where the trouble is. They will not want for aid from the men who think—the men who hold self vastly inferior to principle and justice—the rare noblemen of nature, honorable, fair, just, tender, and thoughtful men—men who love to see the weakest share with them the benefits of freedom—men who know that they are not the less men because they are tender, that women are not the less women because they are strong; and no land under the sky holds so many such as ours.

It seemed to me that the time had come when women should know for themselves what the Bible teaches for them and what the pulpit has upheld; so I have looked it up a little, and although I cannot soil my lips nor your ears with much of it, there is enough, I think, that I may use to make any self-respecting, pure woman blush that she has sustained it by word or act.

The Bible teaches that a father may sell his daughter for a slave, (Ex. xxi. 7) that he may sacrifice her purity to a mob, (Judges xix. 24) and that he may murder her, and still be a good father and a holy man. It teaches that a man may have any number of wives; that he may sell them, give them away, or change them around, and still be a perfect gentleman, a good husband, a righteous man, and one of God's most intimate friends; and that is a pretty good position for a beginning. It teaches almost every infamy under the heavens for woman, and it does not recognize her as a self-directing, free human being. It classes her as property, just as it does a sheep: and it forbids her to think, talk, act, or exist, except under conditions and limits defined by some priest.

If the Bible were strictly followed, women and negroes would still be publicly bought and sold in America. If it were believed in as it once was, if the Church had the power she once had, I should never see the light of another day, and your lives would be made a hell for sitting here to-night. The iron grasp of superstition would hold you and your children forever over the bottomless pit of religious persecution, and cover your fair fame with infamous slander, because you dared to sit here and hear me strike a blow at infinite injustice.

Every injustice that has ever been fastened upon women in a Christian country has been "authorized by the Bible" and riveted and perpetuated by the pulpit. That seems strong language, no doubt; but I shall give you an opportunity to decide as to its truth. I will now bring my witnesses. They are from the "inspired word" itself, and therefore must be all that could be desired. I will read you a short passage from Exodus xx. 22; xxi. 7-8:

*22 And the LORD said unto Moses, Thus thou shalt say unto the children of Israel, Ye have seen that I talked with you from heaven. * * **

7. And if a man sell his daughter to be a maid-servant, she shall not go out as the men-servants do. 8. If she please not her master, who hath betrothed her to himself, then shall he let her be redeemed: to sell her unto a strange nation he shall have no power, seeing he hath dealt deceitfully with her.

The Lord doesn't object to a man selling his daughter, but if any one thing makes him angrier than another it is to have her go about as the men-servants do after she is sold. On a little point like that he is absolutely fastidious. You may here notice that God took the trouble to come down from heaven to tell the girl what not to do after she was sold. He forgot to suggest to her father that it might be as well not to sell her at all. He forgot that. But in an important conversation one often overlooks little details. The next is Joshua xv. 16-17:

16 And Caleb said, He that smiteth Kirjath-sepher, and taketh it, to him will I give Achsah my daughter to wife. 17 And Othniel the brother of Caleb [and consequently the girl's uncle] took it: and he gave him Achsah his daughter to wife.

Please to remember that the said Caleb was one of God's intimates—a favorite with the Almighty. The girl was not consulted; the father paid off his warriors in female scrip. The next is Gen. xix. 5-8:

*5 And they called unto Lot, and said unto him, Where are the men which came in to thee this night? bring them out unto us that we may know them. 6 And Lot went out at the door unto them, and shut the door after him. 7 And said, I pray you, brethren, do not so wickedly. 8 Behold now, I have two daughters * * * * let me, I pray you, bring them out unto you, and do ye to them as is good in your eyes; only unto these men do nothing; for therefore came they under the shadow of my roof.*

These men had come under the shadow of Lot's roof for protection, it seems, and Lot felt that his honor demanded that he should shield them even at the cost of the purity and safety of his own daughters! Do you know I have always had a mild curiosity to know what his daughters were under the shadow of his roof for. It could not have been for protection, I judge, since Lot was one of God's best friends. He was on all sorts of intimate terms with the Deity—knew things were going to happen before they came—

was the only man good enough to save from a doomed city—the only one whose acts pleased God and this act seems to have been particularly satisfactory. These men were "angels of God" who required this infamy for their protection! If it takes all the honor out of a man when he gets to be an angel, they may use my wings for a feather-duster. Now here is a little property law. Num. xxvii:

6 And the LORD spake unto Moses, saying,… 8 And thou shalt speak unto the children of Israel, saying, If a man die, and have no son, then ye shall cause his inheritance to pass unto his daughter.

And our law works a little that way yet; being the result of ecclesiastical law it naturally would. Next we have Num. xxxvi:

8 And every daughter that possesseth an inheritance in any tribe of the children of Israel, shall be wife unto one of the family of the tribe of her father, that the children of Israel may enjoy every man the inheritance of his fathers. 9 Neither shall the inheritance remove from one tribe to another tribe; but every one of the tribes of the children of Israel shall keep himself to his own inheritance. 10 Even as the LORD commanded Moses, so did the daughters of Zelophehad.

That is all the women were for—articles of conveyance for property. Save the land, no matter about the girls. Now these silly women actually believed that God told Moses whom they had to marry just because Moses said so! I tell you, ladies and gentlemen, it is not safe to take heavenly communications at second-hand. Second-hand articles are likely to be varnished over, and have to be taken at a discount. And it seems to me that, if the lord is at all particular as to whom a girl should marry she is the one for him to discuss the matter with. Moses didn't have to live with the sons of Zelophehad, and consequently wasn't the one to talk the matter over with. But, you see, it won't do to question what Moses said God told him, because upon his veracity the whole structure is built. He had more personal interviews with the Deity than any other man—he and Solomon—and hence they are the best authority.

I have here the 31st chapter of Numbers, but it is unfit to read. It tells a story of shame and crime unequalled in atrocity. It tells that God commanded Moses and Eleazar, the priest, to produce vice and perpetrate crime on an unparalleled scale. It tells us that they obeyed the order, and that 16,000 helpless girls were dragged in the mire of infamy and divided amongst the victorious soldiers. They were made dissolute by force, and by direct command of God!

This one chapter stamps as false, forever, the claim of inspiration for the Bible. That one chapter would settle it for me. Do you believe that God told Moses that? Do you believe there is a God who is a thief, a murderer, and a defiler of innocent girls? Do you believe it? Yet this religion is built upon Moses' word, and woman's position was established by him. It seems to me time for women to retire Moses from active life. Coax him to resign on account of his health. Return him to his constituency. He has been on the supreme bench long enough. Don't let your children believe in such a God. Better let them believe in annihilation. Better let them think that the sleep of death is the end of all! Better, much better, let them believe that the tender kiss at parting is the last of all consciousness for them, and after that eternal rest! Don't let their hearts be seared, their lives clouded, their intellects dwarfed by the cruel dread of the God of Moses! Better, thrice better, let the cold earth close over the loved and loving dust forever, than that it should enter the portals of infinite tyranny. Next we will take Deut. xx. 10-16:

10 When thou comest nigh unto a city to fight against it, then proclaim peace unto it. (Good scheme!) 11 And it shall be, if it make thee answer of peace, and open unto thee, then it shall be, that all the people that is found therein shall be tributaries unto thee, and they shall serve thee. 12 And if it will make no peace with thee, but will make war against thee, then thou shalt besiege it: 13 And when the Lord thy God hath delivered it into thy hands, thou shalt smite every male thereof with the edge of the sword: 14 But the women, and the little ones, and the cattle, and all that is in the city, even all the spoil thereof, shalt thou take unto thyself; and thou shalt eat the spoil of thy enemies, which the LORD thy God hath given thee. 15 Thus shalt thou do unto all the cities which are very far off from thee, which are not of the cities of these nations. 16 But of the cities of these people, which the LORD thy God doth give thee for an inheritance, thou shalt save alive nothing that breatheth.

The injunction to proclaim peace unto a city about to be attacked and plundered strikes me as a particularly brilliant idea. When you go to rob and murder a man, just tell him to keep cool and behave like a gentleman and you won't do a thing to him but steal all his property and cut his throat and retire in good order. God always seemed to fight on the side of the man who would murder most of his fellow-men and degrade the greatest number of women. He seemed, in fact, to rather insist on this point if he was particular about nothing else. And, by the way, if you had happened to live in one of those cities, what opinion do you think you would have had of Jehovah? Would he have impressed you as a loving Father? Here we have 2 Samuel v. 10, 12-13:

10 And David went on, and grew great, and the LORD God of hosts was with him. 12 And David perceived that the LORD had established him king over Israel, and that he had exalted his kingdom for his people Israel's sake. 13 And David took him more concubines and wives out of Jerusalem, after he was come from Hebron: and there were yet sons and daughters born to David.

The nearer he got to God—the more God was "with him,"—the more wives he wanted. Next we have 2 Samuel xx. 3:

3 And David came to his house at Jerusalem, and the king took the ten women, his concubines, whom he had left to keep the house, and put them in ward, and fed them . . . . So they were shut up unto the day of their death, living in widowhood.

Now what did David do that for? I don't know. It was such a trifling little matter that it was not thought necessary to give any reason. Perhaps he had eaten too much pie and felt cross; and what else were those women for but to be made to stand around on such occasions? Weren't they his property? Didn't those ten women belong to David? Hadn't he a perfect right to shut them up and feed them if he wanted to? Don't you think it was kind of him to feed them? I wonder if he sang any of his psalms to them through the key-hole. His son Absalom had just been killed, and he felt miserable about that. He had just delivered himself of that touching apostrophe we often hear repeated from the pulpit to-day, to awaken sympathy for God's afflicted prophet: "O my son Absalom, my son, my son Absalom I would God I had died for thee, O Absalom, my son, my son!" And I haven't a doubt that there were at least ten women who echoed that wish most heartily. It must have been carried in the family without a dissenting vote.

To this God of the Bible a woman may not go unless her father or husband consents. She can't even promise to be good without asking permission. This God holds no communication with women unless their male relations approve. He wants to be on the safe side, I suppose. I'll read you about that. It is in one of the chapters that are not commonly cited as evidence that God is no respecter of persons, and that the Bible holds woman as man's equal; nevertheless it is as worthy of belief as any of the rest of it, and its "Thus saith the Lord" and "I as the Lord commanded Moses" are "frequent and painful and free," as Mr. Bret Harte might say. The chapter is Numbers xxx:

And Moses spake unto the heads of the tribes concerning the children of Israel, saying, This is the thing which the LORD hath commanded. 2 If a man vow a vow unto the Lord, or swear an oath to bind his soul with a bond; he shall not break his word, he shall do according to all that proceedeth out of his mouth. 3 if a woman also vow a vow unto the LORD, and bind herself by a bond, being in her father's house in her youth; 4 And her father hear her vow, and her bond wherewith she hath bound her soul, and her father shall hold his peace at her; then all her vows shall stand, and every bond wherewith she hath bound her soul shall stand. 5 But if her father disallow her in the day that he heareth; not any of her vows, or of her bonds wherewith she hath bound her soul, shall stand: and the LORD shall forgive her, because her father disallowed her. 6 And if she had at all an husband when she vowed, or uttered aught out of her lips, wherewith she bound her soul; 7 And her husband heard it, and held his peace at her in the day that he heard it; then her vows shall stand, and her bonds where-

with she bound her soul shall stand. 8 But if her husband disallowed her on the day that he heard it; then he shall make her vow which she vowed, and that which she uttered with her lips, wherewith she bound her soul, of none effect: and the LORD shall forgive her 9 But every vow of a widow, and of her that is divorced, where-with they have bound their souls, shall stand against her. 10 And if she vowed in her husband's house, or bound her soul by a bond with an oath; 11 And her husband heard it, and held his peace at her, and disallowed her not; then all her vows shall stand, and every bond wherewith she bound her soul shall stand. 12 But if her husband hath utterly made them void on the day he heard them; then whatsoever proceeded out of her lips concerning her vows, or concerning the bond of her soul, shall not stand: her husband hath made them void; and the LORD shall forgive her. 13 Every vow, and every binding oath to afflict the soul, her husband may establish it, or her husband may make it void. 14 But if the husband altogether hold his peace at her from day to day; then he establisheth all her vows, or all her bonds, which are upon her: he confirmeth them, because he held his peace at her in the day that he heard them. 15 But if he shall any ways make them void after that he hath heard them; then he shall bear her iniquity. 16 These are the statutes, which the LORD commanded Moses, between a man and his wife, between the father and his daughter, being yet in her youth in her father's house.

Between man and his God they tell us there is no one but a Redeemer; but between woman and man's God there seems to be all her male relations, which, I should think, would prevent any very close intimacy. And by the time the divine commands to woman were filtered through the entire male population, from Moses to the last gentleman who in the confusion natural to the occasion, misquotes "with all thy worldly goods I me endow," I should think it not impossible that some slight errors may have crept in, and the Church should not feel offended if I were to aid her in their detection.

Here we have two or three passages that are said to be the words of Jesus. I hope that is not true. But I, believing him to have been a man, can understand how they might have been the words

of even a very good man in that age and with his surroundings;
but the words of a perfect being—never! Of course I know that we
have no positive knowledge of any of the words of Jesus, since no
one pretends that they were ever written down until long after his
death; but I am dealing now with the theological creation upon
the theologian's own grounds. My own idea of Jesus places him far
above the myth that bears his name.

*3 And when they wanted wine, the mother of Jesus saith unto him,
They have no wine. 4 Jesus saith unto her, woman, what have I to do
with thee?—John ii, 3-4.*

I hope that Christ did not say that—for his manhood I hope
so. I would rather believe that this is the mistake of some "uninspired" writer than think that one who in much had so gentle and
tender a nature, was unkind and brutal to his mother. No one
would attempt, in this age, to apologize for such a reply to so
simple a remark made by a mother to her son. But they say "he
was divine." They also tell us he was a perfect example; but with
this evidence before me, I am glad our men are human. Still I
cannot pretend to say that this is not divine—never having made
any divine acquaintances. I can only say, humanity is better.

Then again he is reported to have said a most cruel thing to
the broken-hearted mother of a dying child, and I would rather
believe the Bible uninspired and keep my respect for Jesus, the
man. It will be better for this world to believe in Jesus, the brave,
earnest man, than in Jesus, the cruel God.

*21 Then Jesus went thence, and departed into the coasts of Tyre
and Sodom [sic]. 22 And behold, a woman of Canaan came out of the
same coasts, and cried unto him, saying, Have mercy on me, O Lord,
thou Son of David; my daughter is grievously vexed with a devil. 23 But
he answered her not a word . . . 25 Then came she and worshiped him,
saying, Lord, help me. 26 But he answered and said, It is not meet to
take the children's bread, and to cast it to dogs. 27 And she said, Truth,
Lord: yet the dogs eat of the crumbs which fall from their masters' table.—
Matt. xv.*

Do you think that was kind? Do you think it was godlike?

What would you think of a physician, if a woman came to him distressed and said, "Doctor, come to my daughter; she is very ill. She has lost her reason, and she is all I have!" What would you think of the doctor who would not reply at all at first, and then, when she fell at his feet and worshiped him, answered that he did not spend his time doctoring dogs? Would you like him as a family physician? Do you think that, even if he were to cure the child then, he would have done a noble thing? Is it evidence of a perfect character to accompany a service with an insult? Do you think a man who could offer such an indignity to a sorrowing mother has a perfect character, is an ideal God? I do not. And I hope that Jesus never said it. I prefer to believe that that story is a libel.

It won't do. We have either to give up the "inspiration" theory of the Bible, and acknowledge that it is the work of men of a crude and brutal age, and like any other book of legend and myth of any other people; or else to give up the claim that God is any better than the rest of us. You can take your choice.

Whenever a theologian undertakes to explain matters so as to keep the Bible and the divine character both intact, I am always reminded of the story of the Irishman who was given a bed in the second story of a lodging-house the first night he spent in New York. In the night the fire-engines ran past with their frightful noise. Aroused from a deep sleep and utterly terrified, Mike's first thought was to get out of the house. He hastily jerked on the most important part of his costume, unfortunately wrong side before, and jumped out of the window. His friend ran to the window and exclaimed, "Are ye kilt, Mike?" Picking himself up and looking himself over by the light of the street lamp, he replied, "No, not kilt, Pat, but I fear I am fatally twisted."

Next we have God's opinion (on Bible authority) as to the use of wives. They were to be forcibly changed around as a Punishment to their husbands and for offenses committed by the latter.

11 Thus saith the LORD, Behold, I will raise up evil against thee out of thy own house, and I will take thy wives before thy eyes and give them unto thy neighbor.—2 Sam. xii.

The latter part of the verse is omitted as being unfit to read. Don't understand that I think any of it is exactly choice literature; but that cover has been used to silence objection long enough. If it is fit to teach as the word and will of God for women, it ought to be fit to read in a theater—but it is not.

What do you think of a religion that upholds such morals and such justice as that just quoted? What do you think of women supporting the Bible in the face of that as the will of God? Of all human beings a woman should spurn the Bible first. She, above all others, should try to destroy its influence; and I mean to do what little I can in that direction. The morals of the nineteenth century have outgrown the Bible. Jehovah stands condemned before the bar of every noble soul. What Moses and David and Samuel taught as the word and will of God, we, who are fortunate enough to live in the same age with Charles Darwin, know to be the expression of a low social condition untempered by the light of science. Their "thus saith the Lord," read in the light of to-day, is "thus saith ignorance and fear"—no more, no less.

If you will read the 12th chapter of Leviticus, which is unfit to read here, you will see that the Bible esteems it twice as great a crime to be the mother of a girl as to be the mother of a boy; so highly esteemed was woman by the priesthood; so great a favorite was she of Jehovah.

And do you know there is a law in the Bible which "the Lord spake unto Moses" that says if a man is jealous of his wife, "whether he have cause or not," he is to take her to a priest, and take a little barley meal (if you ever want to try it, remember it must be barley meal; I don't suppose the priest could tell whether she was guilty or not if you were to take corn meal or hominy grits) and put it in the wife's hands. And the priest is to take some "holy" water and scrape up the dirt off the floor of the Tabernacle, and put the dirt in the water and make the wife drink it. Now just imagine an infinite God getting up a scheme like that! Then the priest curses her and says if she is guilty she shall rot. . . . "and she shall say Amen." That is her defence! Then the priest takes the stuff she has

in her hands—this barley-meal "jealousy offering"—and "waves it
before the Lord." (I suppose you all know what that part is done
for. If you don't, ask some theological student with a number six
hat-band; he'll tell you.) And then he burns a pinch of it (that is
probably for luck), and at this point it is time to make the woman
drink some more of the filthy water (which he does with great
alacrity), and "if she be guilty the water will turn bitter within
her," . . . "and she shall be accursed among her people." (You
doubtless perceive that her defence has been most elaborate
throughout.) Do you think that water would be bitter to the priest?

But if she does not complain that the water is bitter, and if her
"Amen" is perfectly satisfactory all round, and she be pronounced
innocent, what then? Is the husband in any way reproved for his
brutality? Did the Lord "reveal" to Moses that he should drink the
rest of that holy water and dirt? No! That wasn't in Moses' line.
Neither he nor the husband drink the rest of that water—priest
doesn't either; they don't even take a pinch of the barley. But after
she is subjected to this, and the show is over, "if she be innocent,
then shall she go free!" Oh, ye gods! what magnificent generosity!
I should have thought they would have hanged her then for being
innocent.

*"And then shall the man be guiltless of iniquity, and the woman
shall bear her iniquity."*

If she is innocent she shall bear her iniquity. You all see how
that is done I suppose. If you don't, ask your little number six
theological student, and he will tell you all about it, and he will
also prove to you, without being asked, that he and God are capable
of regulating the entire universe without the aid of General Butler.

But I am told that I ought to respect and love the Bible that
all women ought to take an active part in teaching it to the heathen, to show them how good Jehovah is to his daughters. But if
he is, he has been unusually unfortunate in his choice of executors.

Nor is it only in the Old Testament that such morals and such
justice are taught. The clergy put that part off by saying—"Oh,
that was a different dispensation, and God, the Unchangeable, has

changed his mind." That is the sole excuse they give for all the "holy" men, who used to talk personally with God, practicing polygamy and all the other immoralities. They maintain that it was God's best man who upheld polygamy then, and that it is the Devil's best man who does it now. Odd idea isn't it? Simply a question of time and place; and as Col. Ingersoll says, you have got to look on a map to see whether you are dammed or not. But it does seem to me that a God that did not always know better than that, is not a safe chief magistrate. He might take to those views again. They say history is likely to repeat itself. Anyhow, I would rather be on the safe side and just fix the laws so that he couldn't. It would be just as well.

But now we have come to "St." Paul and his ideas on the woman question. He worked the whole problem by simple proportion and found that man stands in the same relation to woman as God stands to man. That is, man is to woman as God is to man—and only a slight remainder. I'm not going to misrepresent this gifted saint. I shall let him speak for himself. He does it pretty well for a saint, and much more plainly than they usually do.

22 Wives, submit yourselves unto your own husbands, as unto the Lord. 23 For the husband is the head of the wife, even as Christ is the head of the church: and he is the savior of the body.—Ephesians v.

The husband is the savior of the wife! Pretty slim hold on heaven for most women, isn't it? And then suppose she hasn't any husband. Her case is fatal.

24 Therefore as the church is subject unto Christ, so let the wives be to their own husbands in everything.—Ephesians v.

Paul was a modest person in his requirements.

9 In like manner also, that women adorn themselves in modest apparel, with shamefacedness and sobriety; not with braided hair, or gold, or pearls, or costly array.—I Timothy ii.

It does seem as if anybody would know that braided hair was wicked; and as to "gold and pearls and costly array," all you have to do to prove the infallibility of Paul—and what absolute faith Christians have in it!—is to go into any fashionable church and observe the absence of all such sinfulness:

10 But (which becometh women professing godliness) with good works. 11 Let the woman learn in silence with all subjection. 12 But I suffer not a woman to teach, nor to usurp authority over the man, but to be in silence. 13 For Adam was first formed, then Eve. 14 And Adam was not deceived, but the woman being deceived was in the transgression.—I Timothy ii.

According to the reasoning of verse 13 man should be subject to all the lower animals, because they were first formed, and then Adam. Verse 14 tells us that Adam sinned knowingly; Eve was deceived, so she deserves punishment. Now I like that. If you commit a crime understandingly it is all right. If you are deceived into doing it you ought to be damned. The law says, "The criminality of an act resides in the intent"; but more than likely St. Paul was not up in Blackstone and did not use Coke.

This next is St. Peter, and I believe this is one of the few topics upon which the infallible Peter and the equally infallible Paul did not disagree:

Likewise, ye wives, be in subjection to your own husbands; that, if any obey not the word, they also may without the word be won by the conversation of the wives; 2 While they behold your chaste conversation coupled with fear.—1 Peter iii.

I should think that would be a winning card. If the conversation of a wife, coupled with a good deal of fear, would not convert a man, he is a hopeless case.

But here is Paul again, in all his mathematical glory, and mortally afraid that women won't do themselves honor.

3 But I would have you know, that the head of every man is Christ; and the head of the woman is the man; and the head of Christ is God. 4 Every man praying or prophesying, having his head covered, dishonoreth his head. 5 But every woman that prayeth or prophesieth with her head uncovered, dishonoreth her head; for that is even all one as if she were shaven. 6 For if the woman be not covered, let her also be shorn: but if it be a shame for a woman to be shorn or shaven, let her be covered. 7 For a man indeed ought not to cover his head, forasmuch as

he is the image and glory of God: but the woman is the glory of the
man: 8 For the man is not of the woman, but the woman of the man.
9 Neither was the man created for the woman, but the woman for the
man.—1 Cor. xi.

And that settles it, I suppose. But what on earth was man
created for? I should not think it could have been just for fun.

34 Let your women keep silence in the churches; for it is not per-
mitted unto them to speak but they are commanded to be under obedi-
ence, as also saith the law. 35 And if they will learn anything, let them
ask their husbands at home: for it is a shame for women to speak in the
church.—1 Cor. xiv.

That is a principle that should entitle St. Paul to the profound
admiration of women. And yet, when I come to think of it, I don't
know which one gets the worst of that either. Whenever you want
to know anything, ask your husband, at home! No wonder most
husbands don't have time to stay at home much. No wonder they
have to see a man so often. It would unseat any man's reason if he
lived in constant fear that he might, any minute, be required to
explain to a woman of sense, how death could have been brought
into this world by Eve, when every one knows that long before
man could have lived upon this earth animals lived and died. It
would make any man remember that he had to "catch a car" if he
were asked suddenly to explain the doctrine of the Trinity. I would
not blame the most sturdy theologian for remembering that it was
club night, if his wife were to ask him, unexpectedly, how
Nebuchadnezzar, with his inexperience, could digest grass with
only one stomach, when it takes four for the oxen that are used to
it. That may account, however, for his hair turning to feathers.

I don't believe St. Paul could have realized what a diabolical
position he was placing husbands in, when he told wives to ask
them every time they wanted to know anything—unless he wanted
to make marriage unpopular. There is one thing certain, he was
careful not to try it himself, which looks much as if he had some
realizing sense of what he had cut out for husbands to do, and felt

that there were some men who would rather be drafted—and then send a Substitute.

But why are his commands not followed to-day? Why are not the words, sister, mother, daughter, wife, only names for degradation and dishonor?

Because men have grown more honorable than their religion, and the strong arm of the law, supported by the stronger arm of public sentiment, demands greater justice than St. Paul ever dreamed of. Because men are growing grand enough to recognize the fact that right is not masculine only, and that justice knows no sex. And because the Church no longer makes the laws. Saints have been retired from the legal profession. I can't recall the name of a single one who is practicing law now. Have any of you ever met a saint at the bar?

Women are indebted to-day for their emancipation from a position of hopeless degradation, not to their religion nor to Jehovah, but to the justice and honor of the men who have defied his commands. That she does not crouch to-day where Saint Paul tried to bind her, she owes to the men who are grand and brave enough to ignore St. Paul, and rise superior to his God.

And remember that I have not read you the worst stories of the Bible. The greater number of those which refer to women are wholly unfit to read here. Are you willing to think they are the word of God? I am not. Believe in a God if you will, but do not degrade him by accepting an interpretation of him that would do injustice to Mephistopheles! Have a religion if you desire, but demand that it be free from impurity and lies, and that it be just. Exercise faith if you must, but temper it wisely with reason. Do not allow ministers to tell you stories that are sillier than fairy tales, more brutal than barbaric warfare, and too unclean to be read, and then assure you that they are the word of God. Use your reason; and when you are told that God came down and talked to Moses behind a bush, and told him to murder several thousand innocent people; when you are told that he created a vast universe and filled it with people upon all of whom he placed a never-ending curse because of a trivial disobedience of one; give him the benefit of a reasonable doubt and save your reputation for slander.

Now just stop and think about it. Don't you think that if a God had come down and talked to Moses he would have had something more important to discuss than the arrangement of window curtains and the cooking of a sheep? Since Moses was the leader of God's people, their lawgiver, the guardian of their morals, don't you think that the few minutes of conversation could have been better spent in calling attention to some of the little moral delinquencies of Moses himself? Don't you think it would have been more natural for an infinite and just ruler to have mentioned the impropriety of murdering so many men, and degrading so many young girls to a life worse than that of the vilest quarter of any infamous dive, than to have occupied the time in trivial details about a trumpery jewel-box? Since God elected such a man as Moses to guide and govern his people, does it not seem natural that he would have given more thought to the moral worth and practices of his representative on earth, than to the particular age at which to kill a calf? If he were going to take the trouble to say anything, would it not seem more natural that he should say something important?

In his numerous chats with Solomon, don't you think he could have added somewhat to that gentleman's phenomenal wisdom by just hinting to him that he had a few more wives than were absolutely necessary? He had a thousand we are told, which leaves Brigham Young away behind. Yet there are Christians to-day who teach their children that Solomon was the wisest man who ever lived, and that Brigham Young was very close to the biggest fool. It is not strange that some of these children infer that the trouble with Brigham was that he had not wives enough, and that if he had only married the whole state of Massachusetts he and Solomon would now occupy adjoining seats on the other shore, and use the same jew's-harp?

Do you believe for one moment that a God ever talked with any man and told him to murder a whole nation of men, to steal their property, to butcher in cold blood the mothers, and to give the young girls to a camp of brutal soldiers—and that he helped to do it? Do you believe any God ever told a man to give so many of those girls to one tribe, so many to another, and to burn so many as an offering to himself? Do you believe it? I don't. Would you worship him if he had? I would not.

And yet it is true that he did help in such work, or else the word of Moses is not worth a nickel. God did this, or else our religion is founded upon a fraud. He did it, or orthodoxy is a mistake. He did it, or the Bible is an imposition. If it is true, no woman should submit to such a fiend for an hour; if it is false, let her unclasp the clutches of the superstition which is built upon her dishonor and nourished by her hand.

They say it is a shame for a woman to attack the Bible. I say she is the one who should do it. It is she who has everything to gain by its overthrow. It is she who has everything to lose by its support. They tell me it is the word and will of God. I do not, I cannot, believe it! And it does seem to me that nothing but lack of moral perception or mental capacity could enable any human being who was honest (and not seared) to either respect or believe in such a God.

As a collection of ingenious stories, as a record of folly and wickedness, as a curious and valuable old literary work, keep the Bible in the library. But put it on the top shelf—or just behind it, and don't let the children see it until they are old enough to read it with discrimination. As a mythological work it is no worse than several others. As a divine revelation it is simply monstrous.

Among your other tales you might tell the children some from it. You might tell them that at one time a man got mad at another man, and caught three hundred foxes, and set fire to their tails (they standing still the while), and then turned them loose into the other man's corn, and burnt it all up. If they don't know much about foxes, and have never experimented in burning live hair, they may think it is a pretty good story. But I would not tell them that the man who got up that torch-light procession was a good man. I would not tell them that he was one of God's most intimate friends; because even if they think he had a right to burn his enemy's crops, I don't believe that any right-minded child would think it was fair to the foxes.

Some time ago I went to hear a noted minister, who preached a sermon about the "fruit of the tree of knowledge" to a congregation composed, as most congregations are, chiefly of women. Yet his sermon was a monument of insult, bigotry, and dogmatic intolerance that would have done honor to a witch-hunter several centuries ago. That women will subject themselves to such insults week after week, and that there are still men who will condescend to offer them, is a sad commentary upon their self-respect as well as upon the degrading influence of their religion.

Why will they listen to such nonsense? Perhaps woman was made of a rib and so should be held as flesh and blood only, devoid of intellect. But I don't know that she was; I was not there to see, and, in fact, none of my family were; and since they tell us that the only gentleman present upon that interesting occasion was asleep, I don't know who could have told the story in the first place.

It is always a surprise to me that women will sit, year after year, and be told that, because of a story as silly and childish as it is unjust, she is responsible for all the ills of life; that because, forsooth, some thousands of years ago a woman was so horribly wicked as to eat an apple she must and should occupy a humble and penitent position, and remain forever subject to the dictates of ecclesiastical pretenders. It is so silly, so childish, that for people of sense to accept it seems almost incredible.

According to the story, she was deceived. According to the story, she believed that she was doing a thing which would give greater knowledge and a broader life, and she had the courage to try for it. According to the story, she first evinced the desire to be more and wiser than a mere brute, and incidentally gave her husband an opportunity to invent the first human lie (a privilege still dear to the heart), a field which up to that time had been exclusively worked by the reptiles. But they never got a chance at it again. From the time that Adam entered the lists, competition was too lively for any of the lower animals to stand a ghost of a chance at it, and that may account for the fact that, from that time to this, nobody has ever heard a snake tell a lie or volunteer information to a woman. The Church has had a monopoly of these profitable perquisites ever since. The serpent never tried it again. He turned woman over to the clergy, and from that time to this they have been the instructors who have told her which apple to bite, and how big a bite to take. She has never had a chance since to change her diet. From that day to this she has had apple pie, stewed apple, dried apple, baked apple, apple-jack, and cider; and this clergy-man that I heard, started out fresh on apple-sauce. He seemed to think—"anything for a change." You would have thought to hear him, that the very worst thing that ever happened to this world was the birth of the desire for knowledge, and that such desire in woman had been the curse of all mankind.

But it seems to me that if in this day of intelligence a minister preaches or acts upon such dogmas, women should scorn him both as a teacher and as a man. If a creed or Church upholds such doctrines they should shun it as they would a pest-house. If all system or any book of religion teaches such principles they should exert every effort to utterly destroy its influence. I want to do what I can to show woman that the mercury of self-respect must fall several degrees at the church door, and that the light of reason must go out.

In this sermon that I speak of, we were warned "not to be wise above that which is written." As if a man should bind his thoughts and knowledge down to what was known, believed, or written in ages past! As though a man should fear and tremble, should hesi-tate to reach out after, to labor to know, all that his intellect and energy can compass. As though to be good he must accept situa-tions, sentiments, ideas ready-made, and dwarf his intellect and bind his mental ability by the capacity of somebody else.

"He that hath ears to hear, let him hear. He that hath eyes to see, let him see."

And he that hath a brain to think, let him think. What is his intellect for! Why is his mind one vast interrogation point? Why should not Eve have grasped with eagerness the fruit of the tree of knowledge?

A taste of the fruit of the tree of knowledge does drive man from the paradise of ignorance, does send him forth a laborer in the vast fields of speculation and thought, where there is no rest, and no possibility of the cessation of labor so long as his energies and his love of truth remain to impel him to the conquest of the infinite domain that lies unexplored beyond.

But would any man sell what is gained in liberty, in strength, in breadth, in conscious superiority, for the delights which every brute has left him in his stagnant paradise of ignorance and rest? What man in this nineteenth century can unblushingly say he would not choose the labor with all its pain, the effort with all its failure, the struggle with all its exhaustion? Why try to bind the human mind by the silly theory that a God requires man to crush out or subject the intellect he has given him? Whatever religion may have gained by such a course, think what morality and progress have lost by it!

What has not woman lost by that silly fable which made her responsible for transgression? Honor her for it! Honor her the more if it was she who first dared the struggle rather than lose her freedom or crush her reason. If she learned first that the price of ignorance and slavery was too great to pay for the luxury of idleness—honor her for it. The acceptance of such contemptible stories, as told by the clergy in all ages and in all religions as the "word of God," has done more to enslave and injure women's intellects, and to brutalize men, than has been done by any other influence; and our boasted superior civilization is not the result of the Christian religion, but has been won step by step in despite of it. For the Church has fought progress with a vindictive bitterness and power found in no other antagonist—from the time, long ago, when it crushed Galileo for daring to know more than its "inspired" leaders could ever learn, down to yesterday, when it raised a wild howl against Prof.

Tyndall for making a simple statement, in itself absolutely incontrovertible.

It had to yield to Galileo as the people grew beyond its power to blind them to his truth. It is yielding every hour to-day to Tyndall from the same dire necessity; while its nimble devotees vie with each other in proclaiming that they thought that way all the time; had neglected to say so (through an oversight); but that it was one of their very strongest holds from the beginning. They have recently told us that modern scientific doctrines (evolution included) are "plainly indicated in the Bible," and that Science has at last worked up towards the comprehension of scriptural truths.

It used to be the fashion to burn the man who got up a new theory or discovered a new law of nature that interfered with the "revelation" theory; but the style now is to go into the mental gymnastic business and "reconcile" the old dogma with the new truth. The only kind of reconciling the Church ever thought of in the days of her power, was to become reconciled to the death of the scientist or thinker. To-day she can take evolution and revelation, shake them up in a theological bag, and then bring them forth so marvelously alike in appearance that their own father would not know them apart. And the rest of us can't recognize them at all.

To-morrow, when she has to yield her whole field to science, she will hasten to assure us that it was only a few mistaken souls who ever objected to Col. Ingersoll's style of theology; and that if we would only interpret the Bible aright (and understood Hebrew) we should at once discover that Col. Ingersoll was the "biggest card" they had yet.

You may not live until that to-morrow; I may not live until that to-morrow; but it is as sure to come as it is certain that the old tenets have yielded one by one before the irresistible march of an age of intelligence and freedom, in which a priest or a Church can no longer be judge, jury, and counsel.

Not long ago I heard two gentlemen—one a very devout Christian—talking about what use the Church could make of Col. Ingersoll's teachings. One said he was such a moral man, and always insisted so strongly upon right action in this world, that it was a pity he did not have more faith. He said, "What a power he would be in the Church! What a preacher he would make! He would be a second St. Paul—I have been praying for years for his conversion." "Well," said the other, "you needn't waste your time any longer; softening of the brain doesn't run in Robert's family."

Let man rid himself of the pernicious idea that knowledge is a crime, and then let only the man who is afraid to enter the world of thought go back to his native paradise of ignorance and rest. Let him cling to his old ideas. Humanity can do better without such a man, and humanity will be better without him. The time is past when his type is needed, and let us hope that it is nearly past when it can be found. He may have been abreast of the time in 1840, but his grave was dug, his epitaph written, in 1841. Science did not wait for him, and the world forgot his name!

Do you think the world has any further use for the man who can gravely tell those stories about Samson, for instance as truth—as the word of God? Do you think they do honor to most attenuated intellect? Now just stop and think of it. Just think of one thousand able-bodied men (1,000 is a good many men) quietly standing around waiting for Samson to knock them on the head with a bone! And how does the durability of that bone strike you?

If prowess with arms were estimated, I should say that was about the most effective piece of generalship on record. If the gentleman who conducted that neat little skirmish were living today there would not be a question as to his eligibility for a third term, unit rule or no unit rule. If we could provide our generals with a bone like that, we might reduce the standing army sufficiently to reassure the most timid congressman of the whole lot. It would not take more than four or five generals and a captain to guard the whole frontier. Then we might keep a private to keep the peace at the polls, and that would give us sufficient force to readily murder several thousand people any morning before breakfast, and I don't see how you could ask for anything better than that. Two live men and one dead mule could raise a siege in a quarter of an hour. Now, if there is anybody who wants to start "a brilliant foreign policy," here is his chance. He could at the same time make a record for economy, for it would be an enormous saving to this country in arms and ammunition alone. For durability, cheapness, and certainty not to miss fire there is simply no comparison at all.

It may be objected that our soldiers are not so strong as Samson; but I am told by those who are intimately acquainted with mules, that they have not deteriorated. They have simply transferred their superior strength and durability from their jaw-bones to their heals—and they engineer them themselves. So if our men can stand his voice and aim him right, they won't have to wear long hair.

But seriously, if it is necessary to believe such stories as that in order to go to heaven, don't you think the admission fee is a trifle high? It is entirely beyond my means, and that is not one of the big stories either.

The one that comes right after it is just as absurd. It is the second scene of the same performance, and Samson only went out between acts for a drink, and then he playfully walked off with a building about the size of the capitol at Washington.

They say we must believe these tales or be damned; and that a woman has not even a right to say, "I object." But it always did seem to me that anybody who could believe them would not have brains enough to know whether he was damned or not. They say we must not laugh at such very solemn things as that. They also say that even if we don't believe them ourselves we should show respect for those who do.

That is a very good theory, but I should like to know how any human being with a sense of humor could sit and look solemn, and feel very respectful, with that sort of chaff rattling down his back. It can't be done unless he is scared. Fear will convince a man the quickest of anything on earth. Even a shadow is provocative of solemnity if the light is dark enough and the man is sufficiently seared.

Ignorance and Fear made the Garden of Eden, they created Jehovah, gave Samson his wonderful strength, and Solomon his wisdom; they divided the Red Sea, and raised Lazarus from the dead.

It is not strange, therefore that they have compelled women to cling to the Church, and slaves to cling to slavery. There were many black men in the South who voluntarily went back and offered to remain in bondage. And that is one of the strongest arguments against the institution of slavery—that it can so far degrade its victims that they lose even the ambition to be free! (NOTE: "It was quite an ordinary fact in Greece and Rome for slaves to submit to death by torture rather than betray their masters. Yet we know how cruelly many Romans treated their slaves. But in truth these intense individual feelings nowhere rise to such a luxuriant height as under the most atrocious institutions. It is part of the irony of life, that strongest feelings of devoted gratitude of which human nature seems susceptible, are called forth in human beings toward those who, having the power entirely to crush their earthly existence, voluntarily refrain from using that power. How great a place in most men this sentiment fills, even in religious devotion, it would be cruel to inquire. We daily see how much their gratitude to Heaven appears to be stimulated by the contemplation of fellow-creatures to whom God has not been so merciful as he has to themselves."—Mill.)

The time is not far distant when a bondage of the intellect to the Church will receive no more respectful consideration than a bondage of the body to a master. This nineteenth century cannot much longer be bound by the ignorance and intolerance of an age when might was the highest law and force the only appeal. We need to recognize that the broadest possible liberty is the greatest possible good; and that the liberty to think is the highest good of all. So don't let people make you afraid to think, or to laugh at nonsense wherever you see it.

Solomon saying it cannot make a silly thing wise, nor Moses doing it a cruel thing kind. David cannot make brutality gentle, nor Paul injustice just; and that the Bible sustains a wrong can never make it right.

Don't you know that if the leading men of the Old Testament were living to-day, they would be known as liars, thieves, and murderers—some indeed as monsters to whom even these terms would be base flattery. Despoilers of those who had not injured them; infamous liars in the name of God; murderers of men; butchers of children; debauchers of women; if they were living in the nineteenth century they would be unanimously elected to the gallows—that is if they escaped Judge Lynch long enough. And yet they are held up to us, who have outgrown their morals, as authorities on the subject of God's will to man, as Prophets, Saints, Mediators!

Do you want your children taught to believe in the purity and honor of such men? Do you want your children taught to worship a God who sanctioned, commanded, and gloried (and usually participated) in their worst crimes? Do you want them to believe that at any time, in any age, a God was the director in the most heinous crimes, in the vilest plots, in the most cruel, vulgar, cowardly acts of vice that were ever recorded? Either he was or else Moses' word is not worth a copper, and theology is the invention of ignorance. He did these hideous things or the Bible is mistaken about it. There is to-day that kind of a God somewhere in space waiting around to pounce on anybody who doesn't admire him, or else the Church is founded upon the ignorance and fear of its dupes, and teaches them what is not true.

They say it is wicked to inquire into the facts. I say it is wrong not to. It seems to me that in a matter like this the most important thing is to be honest all round, and that if the claims of the Church are true no inquiry can injure them. They say, "Oh, well, drop all the bad part, and only take the good. There is a great deal of good in it too." But if I don't know what is good myself I won't go to Moses and that class of men to find out. I'll go to somebody who has got a clean record. I won't go to men who robbed and murdered in the name of God; I won't go to men who bought and sold their fellow-men; I won't go to men who gave their own daughters over to the hate and lust of others, even bargaining for them with sons and brothers. Such men cannot tell me what is good. Such men cannot make a religion for me to live by, or a God that I can accept.

I am sometimes told that intelligent ministers nowadays do not believe in the inspiration of the Bible and do not teach it. Yet every minister who, like the Rev. R. Heber Newton, dares to suggest mildly that even the apple story is a fable, is silenced by his bishop or hounded down for "heresy." And still they go right on telling little children that it is the "word of God" and the only guide of life, For truth, better give them Aesop's Fables or the Arabian Nights; for purity the Decameron or Don Juan; for examples of justice the story of Blue-Beard or the life of Henry the Eighth.

I wish you would read the Bible carefully just as you would any other book, and see what you think of its morals. I am debarred from touching the parts of it that are the greatest insult to purity and the most infamous travesties of justice, I can only say to you, read it, and if you are lovers of purity you will find that it teaches respect for a God who taught the most degrading impurity and defended those who forced it upon others. If you believe in the sacredness of human life, he gave the largest license to murder. It does not matter that Moses said he told him to tell somebody else "Thou shalt not kill;" for the same gentleman remarked upon several other occasions that God told him not only to kill, but to steal, to lie, to commit arson, to break pretty much all the other commandments—and to be a professional tramp besides. (I am told that he followed this latter occupation for forty years, which I should think would give him the belt.) So you see we have the same gentleman's word for all of it; and at times, I must confess, it does not seem to me absolutely reliable authority. There is one thing certain, if the returns are correct, and that is that Moses did not take his own medicine in the little matter of keeping the commandments. They were for his enemies and his slaves.

If you love liberty remember that the Bible teaches slavery in every form, Not only the buying of slaves, but the stealing them into bondage. How any man or woman who censured slavery in our Southern States can permit their children to be taught that the Bible is a book of authority, and think they are consistent, I cannot understand. Every slave-whip had for its lash the Bible. Every slave-holder had its teachings for his guide. Every slave-driver found his authority there. When the sword of the North severed the thongs of the black man, it destroyed the absolute control of the Bible in America and gave a fatal blow to Jehovah the God of oppression. Only in the South is it that the Bible still holds its own. Freedom has outgrown it; and the young South is reading it, for the first time, with an eraser!

If you respect your mother, if you wish your children to respect theirs, you will find that the Bible teaches not only disrespect for her, but abject slavery and the most oppressive degradation. If you love your young sister, your beautiful pure daughter, remember that Jehovah taught that, whenever men could do so, they were to abuse, ruin, degrade them; and remember, further, that his "prophets"—The men who made our religion—did these things and gloried in the work.

It is for this reason that I say it is right and peculiarly fitting that women should object to his teaching. After you have read the 31st chapter of Numbers, with its "thus saith the Lord," think then if you want to follow such teachings. Decide then whether or not the words, the acts, the commands, or the religion of such men is good enough for you. Think then whether or not you want your daughters, your sons, to believe that the Bible has one grain of authority, or is in any sense a revelation of the divine will.

Don't allow ministers to palm off platitudes on you for "revelation"; and don't let them make you believe that anything that Moses or David or Solomon said was the command of God to women. Neither one of those men was fit to speak of a respectable woman. With the superior morals of our time neither one of them would be considered fit to live outside of a brothel.

And don't lot them tell you what "Saint" Paul said either. What did he know about women anyway? He was a brilliant but erratic old bachelor who fought on whichever side he happened to find himself on. He could accommodate himself to circumstances and accept the situation almost as gracefully as that other biblical gentleman who quietly went to housekeeping inside of a whale, and held the fort for three days.

Did it ever occur to you that those absurd tales have as much claim to be called the "word of God" as any of the rest of it? How can people say they believe such nonsense? And how can they think it is evidence of goodness to believe it? They say it takes a horribly wicked man to doubt one of those yarns; and to come right out and say honestly, "I don't believe it," will elect you, on the first ballot, to a permanent seat in the lower house. Mr. Talmage says four out of five Christians "try to explain away" these tales by giving them another meaning, and he urges them not to do it. He says, stick to the original story in all its literal bearings. The advice is certainly honest, but it would take a brave man to follow it. And four out of five of even professed Christians is a pretty heavy balance on the side of intellectual integrity; and even Mr. Talmage's mammoth credulity fails to tip the scale.

They simply can't believe these biblical stories, so they try to explain the marvelous part entirely away. It has about come to this, in this day of thought and intelligence, that when a thinking man claims to believe these tales, and says it is an evidence of righteousness to believe them, there are just two things to examine, his intellect and his integrity. If one is all right the other is pretty sure to be out of repair. Defective intellect or doubtful integrity is what he suffers from. He has got one of them sure, and he may have both.

Now I should just like to ask you one honest question. Why should any book bind us to sentiments that we would not tolerate if they came from any other source? And why tolerate them com-

58   LAURENCE E. DALTON AND SHIRLEY STRUTTON DALTON, ED

ing from it? Do you know who compiled the Bible? Do you know it was settled by vote which manuscripts God did and which he did not write? The ballot is a very good thing to have; but I decline to have it extend its power into eternity, and bind my brain by the capacity of a ballot-box hold by caste and saturated with blood.

There can be but slow progress while we are weighted down by the superstitions of ages past. The brain of the nineteenth century should not be bound down to the capacity of the third, nor its moral sentiment dwarfed to fit Jehovah.

But so long as the theories of revelation and vicarious atonement are taught, we shall not need to be surprised that every murderer who is hanged to-day says that he is going, with bloody hands, directly into companionship with the deity of revelation. He has had ample time in prison to re-read in the Bible (what he had previously been taught in Sunday school), of many worse crimes than his which his spiritual adviser assures him (to the edification and encouragement of all his kind outside) were not only forgiven, but were actually ordered and participated in, by the God he is going to.

That is what orthodoxy tells him! Just think of it! Do you think that is a safe doctrine to teach to the criminal classes? Aside from its being dishonest, is it safe? Does it not put a premium on crime? I maintain that it is always a dangerous religion where faith in a given dogma, and not continuous uprightness of life, is the standard of excellence. It is a cruel religion where force is king and immorality God. It is an unjust religion which seeks to make women serfs and men tyrants. It is an unreasonable religion where credulity usurps the place of intellect and judgment. It is an immoral religion where vice is deified and virtue strangled. It is a cowardly religion where an innocent man, who was murdered 1,800 years ago, is asked to bear the burden of your wrong acts to-day. Aside from its impossibility that is cowardly.

Man should be taught that for every wrong he does, he must himself be responsible—not that some one else stands between him and absolute personal responsibility—not that Eve caused him to sin, nor that Christ stands between him and full accountability for his every act.

And he should be taught that for every noble deed, for every act of justice or mercy, he deserves the credit himself; that Christ does not need it; that Christ cannot want it; and that Christ does not deserve it.

And you will not want to "wash your hands in the blood of Christ," nor to shed that of any other innocent man, if your motives are pure and your lives clean.

VICARIOUS ATONEMENT

In an art collection in Boston there is a god—a redeemer—the best illustration I have ever seen of the vicarious atonement theory. It is a perfect representation of the agony endured by a helpless and innocent being in order to relieve the guilty of their guilt. This god was captured in Central Africa before his mission was complete, and there is still suffering-space upon his body unused.

It is a wooden image of some frightful beast, and it is represented as suffering the most intense physical agony. Nails are driven into its head, body, legs, and feet. Each wrong-doer who wanted to relieve himself of his own guilt drove a nail, a tack, a brad, or a spike into the flesh of his god. The god suffered the pain; the man escaped the punishment. He cast his burdens on his god, and went on his way rejoicing. Here is vicarious atonement in all its pristine glory. The god is writhing and distorted with pain; the criminal has relieved himself of further responsibility, and his faith has made him whole, his sins are forgiven, and his god will assume his load.

It is curious to examine the various illustrations of human nature as represented by the size and shape of the nails. A sensitive man had committed a trifling offence, and he drove a great spike into the head of the god. A thick-skinned criminal inserted a small tack where it would do the least harm—in the hoof. An honest, or an egotistic penitent drove his nail in where it stands out prominently; while the secretive devotee placed his among a mass of others of long standing and inconspicuous location.

One day I stood with a friend looking at this god. My friend, who was a devout believer in the vicarious theory of justification and punishment as explained away by the ethical divines of Boston, was unable to see anything but the most horrible brutality and willingness to inflict pain on the part of these African devotees, and was equally unwilling to recognize the same principle when applied to orthodoxy. She said, "Is it not horrible, the ignorance and superstition of these poor people? What a vast field of labor our missionaries have."

To her the idea of justification by faith in a suffering god meant only superstition and brutality when plainly illustrated in somebody else's religion; but the same idea, the same morality, the same justice, she thought beautiful when applied to Christianity.

I said, "There is the whole vicarious theory in wood and iron." That is exactly the same as the Christian idea; and the same human characteristics are plainly traceable in the size and location of these nails.

A Presbyterian or Methodist drives his nail in the most conspicuous spot, where the flesh is tender and the suffering plainly visible. The Episcopalian or Catholic uses a small tack, and drives it as much out of sight as possible, covering it over with stained glass, and distracting the attention with music; but the bald, cruel, unjust, immoral, degrading, and dishonest principle is there just the same.

"Faith in blind acts of devotion; the suffering of innocence for guilt; transferring of crime; comfort and safety purchased for self by the infliction of pain and unmerited torture upon another; premiums offered for ignorance and credulity; punishments guaranteed for honest doubt and earnest protest—all these beautiful provisions of the vicarious theory are as essential to our missionary's belief as to that of his African converts; and it seems to me simply a choice between thumbs up and thumbs down."

While we were talking my friend's pastor joined us, and she told him what I had said, and asked him what was the difference between the Christian and the heathen idea of a suffering god. He said he could explain it in five minutes some morning when he had time. He said that the one was the true and living faith, and the other was blind superstition. He also said that he could easily make us see which was which. Then he gracefully withdrew with the air of one who says: "In six days God made the heavens and the earth, and on the seventh day he and I rested." He has not called since to explain. While he stayed, however, his manner was deeply solemnly, awfully impressive; and of course I resigned on the spot.

The theory of vicarious atonement is the child of cowardice and fear. It arranges for a man to be a criminal and to escape the consequences of his crime. It destroys personal responsibility, the most essential element of moral character. It is contrary to every moral principle.

The Church never has been and never will be able to explain why a god should be forced to resort to such injustice to rectify a mistake of his own. To earnest questions and honest thoughts it has always replied with threats. It has always silenced inquiry and persecuted thought. Past authority is its god, present investigation its devil. With it brains are below par, and ignorance is at a premium. It has never learned that the most valuable capital in this world is the brain of a scholar.

Every earnest thought, like every earnest thinker, adds something to the wealth of the world. Blind belief in the thought of another produces only hopeless mediocrity. Individual effort, not mere acceptance, marks the growth of the mind. The most fatal blow to progress is slavery of the intellect. The most sacred right of humanity is the right to think, and next to the right to think is the right to express that thought without fear.

Fear is the nearest approach to the ball and chain that this age will permit, and it should be the glorious aim of the thinkers of to-day that so refined and cruel a form of tyranny shall not be left for those who come after us. We owe physical freedom to the intellectual giants of the lost past; let us leave mental freedom to the intellectual children of the future.

Fear scatters the blossoms of genius to the winds, and superstition buries truth beneath the incrustation or inherited mediocrity. Fear puts the fetters of religious stagnation on every child of the brain. It covers the form of purity and truth with the contagion of contumely and I distrust. It warps and dwarfs every character that it touches. It is the father, mother, and nurse of hypocrisy. It is the one great disgrace of our day, the one incalculable curse of our time; and its nurse and hot-bed is the Church.

Because I, a woman, have dared to speak publicly against the dictatorship of the Church, the Church, with its usual force and honor, answers argument with personal abuse. One reply it gives. It is this. If a woman did not find comfort and happiness in the Church, she would not cling to it. If it were not good for her, she in her purity and truth would not uphold it in the face of the undeniable fact that the present generation of thinking men have left it utterly.

You will find, however, that in every land, under every form of faith, in each phase of credulity it is the woman who clings closest and longest to the religion she has been taught; yet no Christian will maintain that this fact establishes the truth of any other belief. (NOTE: "Exactly the same thing may be said of the women in the harem of an Oriental. They do not complain . . . . They think our women insufferably unfeminine."—Mill)

They will not argue from this that women know more of and have a clearer insight into the divine will! If she knows more about it, if she understands it all better than men, why does she not occupy the pulpit? Why does she not hold the official positions in the Churches? Why has she not received even recognition in our system of religion? Who ever heard of a minister being surprised that God did not reveal any of the forms of belief through a woman? If she knows and does the will of God so much better than men, why did he not reveal himself to her and place his earthly kingdom in her hands?

That argument won't do! As long as creed and Church held absolute power there was no question but that woman was a curse, that she was an inferior being, an after-thought. No Church but the Roman Catholic has the decency to recognize even the so-called mother of God! The Church has never offered women equality or justice. Its test of excellence is force. The closer a Church or creed clings to its spirit, the more surely does it assume to dictate to and control woman and to degrade her. The more liberal the creed the nearer does it come to offering individual justice and liberty.

The testimony of our own missionaries, as well as that of many others, assures us that it is not the Turk but his wives who hold fastest to their faith. The woman of the harem, whom we pity because of the injustice of their religious training, are the last to relinquish their god, the most bitter opponents of the infidel or skeptic in their Church, the most devout and constant believers of the faith, and the most content with its requirements. They are the ones who cling to the form even when the substance has departed—and it is so with us!

Among the "heathen" it is the women who are most shocked and offended by the attacks made upon their superstitions by the missionaries whom we pay to go to them and blaspheme their gods and destroy their idols.

Go where you will, read history as you may, and you will find that it is the men who invented religion, and the women who believed in it. They are the last to give it up. The physically weak dread change. Inexperience fears the unknown. Ignorance shuns thought or development. The dependent cannot be brave.

We are all prepared to admit, I think, that, with but few marked exceptions here and there the women of most countries are physically and mentally undeveloped. They have had fear and dependence, the dread enemies of progress and growth, constantly to retard them. Fear of physical harm, fear of social ostracism, fear of eternal damnation. With rare exceptions a child, with a weak body, or any other dependent, will do as he is told; and women have believed to order. They have done so not only in Christianity but in Buddhism, Mohammedanism, Mormonism, and Fetichism [sic]—in each and all of them. Each and all of them being matter of faith, religion was the one subject in which every Church alike claimed ignorance as a virtue; and the women understood that the men understood it as little as they did. It was a field where credulity and a solemn countenance placed all on an intellectual level—and the altitude of the level was immaterial.

Women have never been expected to understand anything; hence jargon about the "testimony of the spirit," the "three in one" absurdity, the "horns of the altar," or the widow's oil miracle was not more empty or unmeaning to her than a conversation about Bonds and Stocks, Political Economy, or Medical Science. She swallowed her religion just as She did her pills, because the doctor told her to, and said there was something wrong with her head—and usually there was.

The past education of woman gave her an outlook which simply embraced a husband or nothing at all, which was often only a choice between two of a kind.

There are a great many women to-day who think that orthodoxy is as great nonsense as I do, but who are afraid to say so. They whisper it to each other. They are afraid of the slander of the Church.

I want to help make it so that they will dare to speak. I want to do what I can to make it so that a mother won't have to evade the questions of her children about the Bible.

I am sometimes asked, "What do you propose to give in place of this comforting faith? It makes people so happy. You take away all this blessing and you give no other in its place. What is your creed?"

It has never seemed to me, that a creed was the staff of life. Man cannot live by creeds alone. I should not object, however, to one that should read something like this:

I believe in honesty.

I believe that a Church has no right to teach what it does not know.

I believe that a clean life and a tender heart are worth more to this world than all the faith and all the gods of Time.

I believe that this world needs all our best efforts and earnest endeavors twenty-four hours every day.

I believe that if our labors were needed in another world we should be in another world; so long as we are in this one I believe in making the best and the most of the materials we have on hand.

I believe that fear of a god cripples men's intellects more than any other influence. I believe that Humanity needs and should have all our time, efforts, love, worship, and tenderness.

I believe that one world is all we can deal with at a time.

I believe that, if there is a future life, the best possible preparation for it is to do the very best we can here and now.

I believe that love for our fellow-men is infinitely nobler, better, and more necessary than love for God.

I believe that men, women, and children need our best thoughts, our tenderest consideration, and our earnest sympathy.

I believe that God can get on just as well without any of these as with them. If he wants anything he can get it without our assis-tance. it is people with limitations, not gods without limitations, who need and should have our aid.

I believe that it is better to build one happy home here than to invest in a thousand churches which deal with a hereafter.

If a life that embraces this line of action does not fit a man for heaven, and if faith in vicarious atonement will, then such a heaven is not worth going to, and its god would be unworthy to make a good man's acquaintance.

But suppose that faith in a myth is destroyed and another mysticism be not set up in its place, what then? If a mother takes her child away from the fire, which it finds beautiful, and believes to be a nice toy, is it necessary for her to give it a kerosene lamp in its place? She destroys a pleasant delusion—a faith and a delight-ful hope and confidence—because she knows its danger and rec-ognizes its false foundation. It is surely not necessary that she should give to the child another delusion equally dangerous and false. She gives it something she knows to be safe; something she under-stands will not burn; something which, though not so bright and attractive to the child at first, gives pleasure without pain, occupa-tion without disaster. Is she cruel or only sensible? If I were to pretend to a knowledge of a divine creed, a superhuman system, I should be guilty of the same dishonesty, the same deception of which I complain in the Church.

I do not know of any divine commands. I do know of most important human ones. I do not know the needs of a god or of another world. I do not know anything about "a land that is fairer than day." I do know that women make shirts for seventy cents a dozen in this one. I do know that the needs of humanity and this world are infinite, unending, constant, and immediate. They will take all our time, our strength, our love, and our thoughts and our work here will be only then began.

Why not, if you believe in a God at all, give him credit for placing you where he wanted you? Why not give him credit for giving you brains and sympathies, as well as the courage to use them. Even if Eve did eat that apple, why should we insist upon having the colic?

I want to see the time come when mothers won't have to explain to their children that God has changed his mind about goodness and right since he used to incite murder; that eighteen hundred years ago he was a criminal with bloody hands and vile, polluted breath; that less than three hundred years ago his greatest pleasure was derived from witnessing the agony of pure young girls burning alive, whose only crime was beauty of face or honesty of thought.

I want it so that she won't allow her children to hear and believe such a statement as Bishop Fallows made not long ago. He said, in effect, that sins of omission are as heinous as those of commission; that Saul committed two sins in his life, and that one of them was a refusal to commit a cold-blooded murder! He spared the life of a conquered enemy! Out of a whole nation he saved one life—and that was a crime, a sin! Bishop Fallows said that God expressly commanded Saul to utterly exterminate that whole nation, and not only the nation but its flocks; and that God took Saul's kingdom from him because he saved the life of one fallen enemy.

That story, I think, is a libel; and I believe that if there is a God he was never such a fiend! And I want it so that no mother will allow her child to hear such an infamous travesty of the character of a Deity who is called good.

I want it so that all the lessons of the week, all the careful training of a wise father or a good mother, will not be antagonized on Sunday by such a statement as the Rev. Mr. Williamson made at a large church convention recently. Speaking of prayer, he said: "We should offer to God, by prayer, our virtue, our purity, and our pious aspirations" (so far I do not object, for if it means anything I fail to grasp it), "for by not doing so we claim self-control, which is displeasing to God!"

I object! The lesson of self-control is precisely what we need. And when we control ourselves and regulate our lives on principles of right and truth, instead of allowing a Church to regulate them through a fear of hell, we shall be a better people, and character will have a chance to grow.

Then this same gentleman added: "We should also give him our vices, our worry, our temper, and our passions, so that he may dispose of them."

Dispose of them yourselves! Don't try to shift your responsibilities on to somebody else. Don't drive your tack into the brain of justice, expecting to save your own soft skull. Don't enervate your strength to do right by accepting the fatal doctrine of vicarious atonement. It weakens every character that it touches.

The doctrine of vicarious atonement is found in some form in most religions, and it is the body and soul of ours. The idea is not a Christian invention. It caused the Carthaginians to put to death their handsomest prisoners if a battle were won, the most promising children of their own nobility if it were lost. They were offerings to appease the gods.

In old times there were peoples who believed that if a chief was guilty of a misdemeanor it was just to punish or enslave any one of his tribe. That was their idea of liberty and justice. If a father committed a crime it could be expiated by the murder of his son. That was the doctrine of vicarious atonement in all its pristine glory. So they adopted that style of justice in our religion, and condemned the whole lot of us to the eternal wrath of God on account of that little indiscretion attributed to Eve. It seems a very little thing for anybody to get so angry at us all about and stay angry so long! It doesn't seem to me that if one of you were to eat every apple I had in my orchard, I should want to murder all the folks that live in Asia Minor. Do you think you would?

In the 11th verse of the 12th chapter of the second book of Samuel it is claimed that God said he was going to be revenged for the crimes of some men by a vile punishment of their wives.

Only a short time ago a man tried that same style of justice in one of our Western towns. He claimed that Smith had alienated the affections of his wife, so he went over to Smith's house and whipped Mrs. Smith! And do you know that the judge who tried that case (not being a good Bible student) actually sent that good, pious man to the house of correction—that man who not only believed in his Bible but lived by it! And just as likely as not that judge will be elected again. Truly we have fallen on degenerate times.

Legal minds outgrew the idea of vicarious punishment long ago. Physical liberty came to have a new meaning, and punishment was awarded more and more where it was due. But the religious mind never outgrows anything. It is born as big as it ever gets. Development is its terror. It abhors a change. It forces you to sin by proxy, to be redeemed by proxy; and the only thing it does permit you to receive at first hand is Hell. That is the only one thing you can't delegate to somebody else.

If you commit no sin, you are responsible for the sins of other people—dead people, too, that you can't look after. If you are good and true and noble—even if you are a Christian—you don't get any credit for it. If there is any one thing above another that God detests it is to have a man try to be grand and noble and true, and then got the credit of it. "To Christ belongs all the honor, the praise, and the glory—world without end, Amen."

But when it comes to the punishment, the vicarious notion doesn't seem to work. There is the one point where you are welcome to your own, and no discount allowed to heavy takers. Hell is always at par and no bail permitted. Even ignorance of the requirements is no excuse. If you did not know any better, somebody else did, and you've got to pay for it.

Now if the vicarious principle is not big enough to go clear round, I'll leave my share off at the other end. If the Church wants to take my hell (vicariously) it is welcome to it. I will let it go cheap.

Awhile ago a man stayed some time at a hotel in New York, and when the time came for him to pay his bill he hadn't the money. Well, the proprietor felt sorry for him and said, "I tell you what I'll do about that bill, I'll throw off half." His guest was overwhelmed by this liberality, and with tears of gratitude said, "I cannot permit you to out do me in generosity; I'll throw off the other half and we'll call it square."

So if the Church desires all the credit, it is also welcome to all the blame. I cannot permit it to outdo me in generosity. But I'd rather be responsible for just my own sins, and then I can regulate them better, and I can take care of my own reward when I get it. I shall not want to deposit it with the clergy. A profit and loss system that is chiefly loss will not pay me.

The doctrines of vicarious atonement and original or inherited sin are the most infamously unjust dogmas that ever clouded the brain of man. They are twin monsters inherited from intellectual pygmies.

Let me read you a little prayer based upon this idea of right. I heard it offered as a thanksgiving tribute. "Oh, God, we do thank thee that thou didst give thy only son to die for us! We thank thee that the innocent has suffered for the guilty, and that through the suffering and death of thy most holy son our sins are blotted out!"

Monstrous! How would that work in a court of justice? What would you think of a person who coolly thanked a judge who had knowingly allowed the wrong man to be hung? What do you think of a code of morals that offers as one of its beautiful provisions the murder of the innocent instead of the punishment of the guilty?

People ask what good I expect to come of an attack on Christianity. They ask me if I think Christianity does any direct harm. Yes! It makes a man unjust to believe in unjust doctrines. Any man who honestly believes in the righteousness of a system of vicarious rewards and punishments is ripe for any form of tyranny. And the more honestly he believes in it the less will he be a good man from principle.

I want men and women to be good and true because it is right towards each other, and not because they are afraid of Hell. Honor towards people in this world, not fear of a fiend in the next—that is my doctrine. That is the way to make men and women strong and brave and noble. Stop telling them they can't be good themselves; teach them that they must do right themselves. Make them self-dependent. Teach them to stand alone. Honor towards others, kindness, and love—these are what make a man a good husband, a noble father—king in his household.

Fear never made any man a gentleman. Fear never made any woman a true wife or a good mother. Fear never covered the pitfalls of vice with anything stronger than the gloss of hypocrisy.

When Reason's torch burned low, Faith led her victims by chains of ignorance into the land of hopeless superstition, and built her temple there.

A religion of faith is simply a question in geography. Keep your locality in mind and you are all right. On the banks of the Red Sea murder and slavery were a religious duty. On the Ganges infanticide is a virtue. In Rome you may steal or lie; you may deceive an innocent young girl and blast her life forever; you may stab your friend in the dark, and you are all right: but if you eat a piece of fried pork on Friday you are a lost man! China arranges her prayers in a machine, and turns her obligations to Deity off with a crank. There is usually more or less intimate relationship between prayer and a crank. Our God loved human sacrifice in Galilee, and rewarded Abraham for it. He abhors it in Pocasset, America, and his followers threaten to hang the only consistent follower of Jehovah who has come amongst them.

If you live in Utah, or had lived in Jerusalem, your most certain hope of salvation would have been the possession of numerous wives. In England or New York more than one is sure damnation.

Lose your bearings and you are a lost man! Make a mistake in your country and your soul is not worth a copper. A traveler is not safe five minutes, and I doubt if an accident policy would cover his case.

God and the Devil have been held accountable for about every crime that ever has been committed, and it has been very largely a geographical question which of the two was responsible. If it was longitude 35 degrees 14' east it was the Lord! If you shifted to longitude 70 degrees 58' west it was the Devil.

When locality becomes the all-important question, we do not wonder at the old lady who felt relieved when the new survey threw her house just across the state line into Ohio, after she had been under the impression that she lived in Indiana. "Well," said she, "I am glad we don't live in Indiana; I always did say it was a very unhealthy state. Now, our doctor's bills won't be so high."

Pocasset, Mass., is in the devil's country, and murder is not safe; it is a crime. Abraham and Saul lived in a healthier climate— in God's congressional district, where murder was above par and decency was out of fashion. Take it all in all, and the devil seems to make the best Governor.

Now it seems to me that Sunday-schools should teach nothing so much as geography, so that a man may not be in doubt as to who is his Secretary of State, and when an order comes from headquarters he may fairly be expected to know whether it is safe to obey—whether obedience means glorification on earth and a home in heaven, or a sprained neck and a bright fire. It seems now that Pocasset is over the line and out of the Lord's clearing.

Now this God either did or he did not believe in and command murder and rapine in the days when he used to sit around evenings and chat with Abraham and Moses and the rest of them. His especial plans and desires were "revealed" or they were not. The ideas of justice and right were higher in those days than they are now, or else we are wiser and better than God, or else the Bible is not his revealed will. You can take your choice. My choice is to keep my respect for divine justice and honor, and let the Bible bear the burden of its own mistakes.

If religion is a revelation, then it is not a growth, and it would have been most perfect in design and plan when it was nearest its birth. Now accepting the Bible theory of Jehovah, we find that when the communications of God were immediate and personal there could have been no mistake as to his will. To deal with it as a growth or evolution toward better things is to abandon the whole tenet of a revealed law of God. But to deal with it as a revelation is to make God a being too repulsive and brutal to contemplate for one moment with respect.

He either did or did not tell those men those things. Which will you accept?

He divided men into two classes. Of one he made tyrants and butchers; of the other, victims. He made woman weak in order that she might be the more easily overcome by vice; helpless, in order that she might the more easily be made the victim of brutal lust! He made children to be the beasts of burden, the human sacrifices, the defenseless property of criminals and fiends. He did these things or the prophets romanced about it, or some one else romanced about them. Which?

If I accept the former alternative, I can have nothing but loathing and contempt for the Deity and his followers. If the latter, it clouds the character of no one. It simply places the ignorance of the past on the same plane with the ignorance of the present. It rescues the reputation of the Infinite at the trifling expense of a few musty fables.

I choose the latter! I prefer to believe either that a few men were themselves deceived, or that they tried to deceive others—it does not much matter which. I prefer to adopt this belief, and so keep the character of even a supposititious God above reproach.

If we accept a God at all let us accept an honest one.

We are asked to be as fair toward the evidence of Bible witnesses as we are toward other evidence. We are told that we believe a great deal that we have never seen, and that we accept it on the word of others; that we have never seen a man hung, but that we believe that men have been hung; we never saw Napoleon's great feats of generalship, but we believe in them because history records them. Why not believe in the Bible as well as in other history? Why not, on the testimony of witnesses, believe that Christ turned water into wine, as readily as that a man was hung? Why not accept the miracle of the loaves and fishes on evidence, as readily as the victories of Napoleon?

Now that line of argument, although it is the one used by and for theological students, is entirely illogical. It will not work with people who think. The cases are not parallel.

We believe the facts of history and the occurrences of to-day not solely on the testimony of others, but because they are in accord with common sense and experience and judgment; because they fall within the range of possibility, and do not antagonize the laws of nature. We know a man can be hung. We know one general may defeat another. We are asked to believe nothing outside of reasonable bounds. Here then the only thing to examine is the credibility of the witnesses.

If, however, our witnesses told us that whenever Napoleon wanted to know the strength of an enemy he flew up over their camp and counted their men; or that when he found too many he prayed down fire from heaven and burned them up, we should dismiss their testimony at once as unworthy of further notice. We should know that they were deceived, or that they were trying to deceive us. We should know that Napoleon's real means of estimating the strength of his enemy were of a different nature, and that he did not resort to the upper air and flit about at will. We should know that no fire was prayed down, and that although soldiers might be told to put their trust in God, the little addition— "and keep your powder dry"—would be the really important part of the command.

So when we are told that wine was made out of water, and bread and fish out of nothing in large quantities, we know that we are listening to statements that simply go out of the field of credible testimony into the realm of supreme credulity. Such assertions require you to believe not only what you have not seen, but what all experience and reason tell you, you never can see. They ask you not only to believe in a past event, but in a past event outside of all reason, beyond all experience, incapable of demonstration, unsupported by nature, opposed to all natural laws—beneath the realm of reason, out of the light of experience, under the shadow of superstition!

The great electric light of the intellect is turned off at the church door. On one day out of every seven the human lamps enter in utter darkness a field of superstition. During six days the light is turned full on the world of commerce, science, art, and literature, and these glow and grow and are examined by its rays. When, however, the signal tolls from the steeple on the seventh day, the light is turned off for that day and for that topic alone; and then there is brought out once more the old tallow candle of ignorance that hides in shadow the cobwebs of undeveloped thought!

Use your noblest powers of thought freely in the bank; strain and develop your ability to improve and control in the engine-room; train and exert your judgment in literature and art, push and brighten and sharpen your reason in science or political economy.

In the practical affairs of life faith will not help you. It is childish and insecure. It will not honor your cheque; it will not prevent the broken engine from hurling its human companion into eternity. It will not prove the rotundity of the earth, nor establish a sound financial basis for a nation. In all such matters it [leads] to nothing but ignorance and disaster. In theology it is the one element of light.

As a test and an aid in this world, it is puerile and trifling; but the depths of the Great Beyond it fathoms to a nicety. It gives no grasp upon the truths of Time; but it is the all-sufficient hold on Eternity. It leads to the discovery of no important principle here; but it holds the keys to the secret chambers of divinity! It is an attribute of childish development now. It is to indicate infinite mental superiority hereafter!

T

It is a strange philosophy which asserts that a faculty which is a hindrance to superiority in this world is the one thing needful for the soul of man!

Give me the brain that dares to think! Give me the mind that grasps with herculean power the rocks that crush the treasures of intellectual growth, and tears them from their foundation! Give me the mind that dares to step from the fallen stones, that leaps from rock to rock past the dark rift torn in the superstitions of ages past, and that, standing on the farthest crag, waits and witches for the breaking light! He can trust his future whose present scorns stagnation.

In olden times—in the times of the Bible—men believed that animals sometimes used human language, and that beasts were wiser than their masters. I'm not now going to question that belief, but still, I don't think that nowadays one-half of us would take the word of a horse on any important subject. You must remember, however, that it took an ass to know an angel at first sight in Baalim's time. Baalim never suspected that there was an angel in his path until that ass told him! In those days, on a little matter like that, the word of any beast seemed to be taken as good evidence.

But let a mule jam his rider's foot against a wall, nowadays, and then lie down under him, and there is not one man in ten who would associate that fact in his mind with the presence of an angel. I suppose, however, there wasn't as much known about mules then as there is now; and most asses were of a more pious turn of mind.

I don't suppose there is one intelligent man in this city who believes that story, and yet he is not a good Christian if he questions it.

Show me a locality where actual belief—where old time orthodoxy—is looked upon as a requisite of good citizenship and standing in society, and you will show me a place where intellectual development and rapid progress have died or gone to sleep!

The most ignorant and backward parts of this great country, the localities where Congress is asking for better and more secular schools to be established as a means of safety to the state, are situated in the very States where orthodoxy holds absolute sway. In those states a man is looked upon as a very dangerous character if he questions the accuracy of that story about those three hot-house plants, Shadrach, Meshach, and Abednego. Yes, the people of that pious region would be afraid of a man who was wicked enough to laugh at that yarn; and yet do you believe there is a man in this city who could make you believe it? And you don't look dangerous either; and I don't think that I do.

It seems that when they used to run ashore for big scare-stories, they just poked up the fire and went into the blast-furnace business—here and hereafter. But—seeing that a furnace—a real one—heated seven times hotter than it takes to melt iron, did not injure those three tropical innocents—did not even singe their eye-brows—it does look a little as if we should stand a pretty fair show with the spiritual fuel they now promise us hereafter. Still I must say I don't believe I should like the climate.

Speaking of Bible arguments, I must tell you of a new one heard recently. A gentleman acquaintance of mine asked a colored woman, who had applied to him for money to help build a colored people's church, whether she thought God was black or white. She replied that the Bible implied that he was black—that it said, "And his wool shall be whiter than snow"; and that white men don't have wool!

Show me a grade of society that buckles its little belt of belief and faith around its members, and you will show me a collection of hopeless mediocres. The thinkers move out or die out. They object to being fossilized. They decline to go down to history as physical members of the nineteenth century, and mental members of the third.

I would rather have the right to put on my monument "She was abreast of her time," than have all the sounding texts and all the feathered tribes chiseled upon it. I would prefer that it be said of me, "She was a good woman because she had a pure heart," than to have this record: "She was a Christian. She was afraid of Hell. She cast her burdens on the Lord, and went to heaven."

You have been told, "Blessed are they who die in the Lord." Rather let us say, "Blessed are they who live clean lives."

But the Church does not allow you to regulate your lives by what you believe to be right. It always did and it always will hate a thinker. It proposes to do the mental labor for great minds by means of brains large enough to hold nothing but Faith. It says, "I cannot and you shall not outgrow the past. The measure of my capacity shall be the limit of your attainment."

The laws of a nation presume to regulate only what you may do. The Church is kind enough to say what you may think. It proposes to control the mental condition of every man and woman for time and eternity, and its first command is that we shall not grow.

It seems to me rather a queer admission to make, but the Church says that a child or a fool knows quite enough for its purpose—and it does not seem to be my place to question that fact. Now that may be all very well for the child and the fool, but it is rather binding on the rest of us.

Once in a while a minister outgrows the doctrines that were big enough for him in his youth; but that minister, though his life be as pure and his character as sweet as a flower, would be safer to be cast into the sea than that this instrument of torture, this court of injustice, should discover that he had laid aside the outfit of his undeveloped years. His mind may have grown to be a giant in strength, but it must be compressed into the nut-shell of superstition—dwarfed to the capacity of intellectual pygmies.

Christ was a thinker, a man of progress, an infidel, a man who outgrew the Church of his time; and the Church of his time crucified him. Those who oppose the spirit of religious stagnation to-day meet the same spirit in the Church that Christ met, and receive the same treatment so far as the law will permit.

It is a sentiment as true as it is beautiful that asks us to reverence the great men, the thinkers of the past; but it is no mark of respect to them to rest forever over their graves. We show our respect and our appreciation better by a spirit of research that reaches beyond them, than by a simple admiration which takes their gifts and dies. The lessons they left were not alone lessons of memory and acceptance, but examples of effort and progress.

A pupil who stops content with his teacher's last words is no great credit either to himself or to his master. If he has learned only to accept, his lesson is only begun; and until he knows that he must investigate, his education is that of a child, his development that of a clown.

It is no compliment to Christ, the man of progress 1800 years ago, that his followers clip the wings of thought. He struck for freedom from ecclesiastical bondage. He added a new link to the chain of intellectual growth, and his followers have riveted it back to the immovable rock of superstition. He offered a key to open the door of individual liberty. They have wrapped it in the folds of ignorance and laid it in the closet of fear. He said in effect, "When you have outgrown the Church, leave it and bless the world." They say, "Leave it and be damned." For what is a Christian to-day without his hell? The chief objection I hear offered to the last arrangements made for us by the revisers is that they left out some of the hell, and gave the part they kept a poetical name.

When the day comes when offenses against the intellect are deemed as great crimes as offenses against the person, intellectual gag-law will meet with no more respect than lynch-law does to-day, and will be recognized as the expression of an undeveloped moral and social condition. Choking an opinion into or out of a man's mind is no more respectable than the same argument applied to his body.

Any form of faith, any religion, that has the vicarious element in it, is an insult to the intellect. It is based upon the idea of a God of revenge, a ruler infamously unjust. It is a system utterly ineffectual without the wanton sacrifice of helpless innocence under fangs of beastly cruelty—a revenge that has no thought of the redress of wrong by its punishment—a revenge that simply requires a victim— and blood!

Even with those two elements of the plan it is still impotent until it has appealed to the bassist [sic] element in every human breast—the willingness to accept happiness that is bought by the agony of another! It is too abjectly selfish and groveling to command the least respect from a noble character or a great, tender soul. It severs the ties of affection without compunction. It destroys all loyalty. It says, "No matter what becomes of my loved ones—those who would die to help me—I must save my soul." Without the use of the microscope, however, such a soul would never know whether if was saved or not.

What sort of a soul would it be that could have a heaven apart from those it loved? It would not be big enough to save, and its heaven would not be good enough to have.

I prefer the philosophy, the dignified loyalty and love for the dead of the old Goth, the captive warrior whom the Christians persuaded to be baptized. As he stood by the font he asked the bishop, "Where are the souls of my heathen ancestors?" The bishop, with great alacrity, replied, "In hell." The brave old warrior, the loyal Goth, drew his skins about him and said, "I would prefer, if you do not object, to go to my people"; and he left unbaptized.

That was heathen philosophy; but I think I prefer it to the Christianity of a devout man, a Sunday-school superintendent, whom I know. He is a great light in a Christian church today. He worships the beautiful provisions of vicarious atonement. He refused his mother her dying wish, and on the following Sunday atoned for the inhuman act by singing with unusual unction, "How gentle God's commands," and reading with devout fervor, "The Lord is my shepherd, I shall not want." His mother, who had the same shepherd, had wanted for much. She even wanted for a stone to mark her grave, because the money she had left for that purpose her holy son thought best to use, vicariously, upon himself. That man believes in the Bible absolutely. He is a good Christian, and he abhors an infidel! He knows he is going to heaven because he has faith in Christ, and Christ had an extra stab on his account. He is willing to take his heavenly home through the blood of Christ, and his earthly one, out of the pockets of a dead mother. The blood of the murdered Nazarene obliterates the infamy of his acts over her dishonored grave.

And this is perfectly consistent! A religion of faith, a religion that gets its good vicariously and shifts its sins and responsibilities on to the past, is a religion that can never elevate character; it simply makes a man more intensely what he was before. It is all self, self, self. Think of the infinitesimal smallness, the irredeemable worthlessness, the unutterable meanness of a soul that could forsake those it had loved, and be happy believing that they were suffering and eternally lost!

Yet who does not know men who go tramping about the country, living on the charity of their dupes, and declaring that "the Lord is their Shepherd, they shall not want!" whose families want for almost every comfort of life? And this is true orthodox doctrine. "Ye shall forsake father, mother, wife, and children," for what?—to "follow me." Think of the infamy of it!

If that is the kind of souls that go to heaven, I shall do all I can to keep mine amongst more respectable spirits. I will go with the Goth. I could suffer in hell (if there were such a place) with those I love, and keep my self-respect.

If I believed I could be happy in heaven with my loved ones in agony below—if I believed it of myself—there is no vile, slime-covered reptile on earth that I would so loathe! Forsake father, mother, husband, children to save my soul! Never! I will go with my people!

This idea of vicarious atonement has encouraged injustice and crime of every kind. Out of eighty-four men who have been hanged recently, seventy-one have gone directly to heaven. They asked the assembled spectators to be as good as they conveniently could, and meet them on the other shore. Their spiritual advisers administered the holy sacrament, and assured them that they were "lambs of the fold," and that a robe and a harp awaited them at the right hand of God.

Just imagine a lamb in a robe, playing on a harp! A lamb with wings, a harp, a long white robe, and golden slippers seems to me an object to arouse the sympathy of a demon. Poor lamb! He would wish himself a goat every hour of the day.

There is an implied crime in the very word vicarious. If it means anything it means the suffering of innocence to atone for guilt. It means that one crime is condoned by the commission of another—a deliberate one. It means that truth must die in order that dishonor may live. It substitutes vengeance for justice. It does not seek to protect society by checking villainy; it seeks the safety of the criminal by a shifting of responsibility. If the framers of human laws were no wiser that the revealers of divine law, no nation could live, no family would be secure, no justice possible.

Not long ago the New York 'Independent' contained an article against Sarah Bernhart, calling her "a lewd woman," and against her play because it did not contain good morals. The same paper contained an article against George Eliot's works, and said that the Mormon Congressman is a disgrace to all America because he is a polygamist. All these things by a man who swallows David and Lot whole, and has Solomon pose as the summit of all wisdom! All this by a man who builds his life on the word of Moses, and denies to others the right to object to his code of morals or his version of heavenly wisdom and divine direction!

I should like a little consistency. The Christian who rails against polygamy, and at the same time poses in morals with a bible in his hand, is a man who saws his own legs from under him, and still expects us to believe that he has legs, which we might possibly do if only our sight were aided by faith. As long as my eyes hold out, I'll stick to unaided vision; after that, spectacles or faith according to circumstances.

When goodness and virtue are measured, not by a book, but by our own acts toward each other; when a man's character is judged by the amount of joy he gives to his household; when a happy laugh from his children and a bright smile from his wife, greet him as often as he comes home; when these are taken as the evidence of a good man, deacons will go out of fashion. Meek, tired, persecuted-looking wives will not listen to a canting husband

and believe that he is a holy man, when they know that he is a bad husband and a tyrannical father.

There is not any way that I know of to make a home happy vicariously. No confession of faith can take pain out of a mother's heart. No "testimony of the spirit" can make love and beauty in a home where "the heathen" hold the first place, and foreign missions get tangled up in the children's hair. No man accustomed to a high intellectual temperature can keep warm by theological fires. No man whose brain is king can ever again recognize the authority of this mere undisciplined sentiment.

As a system Christianity has had its day. Long ago it may have served a good purpose, but after eighteen hundred years it is worn threadbare and useless. If some of its milder tenets still cling to and fit our vast mediocrity, it is equally certain that the intellectual giants have molted it as the birds moult their plumage in a dying year, and have taken on the bright new garments of higher thought, the spring plumage of intellectual liberty.

When I heard that the Bible was going to be revised I felt very glad because I thought there was a wide field of usefulness open to somebody right there; and I concluded to do all I could to help it along. I understood that they wanted the substance retained as it was, with the language made more as we use language now.

So I began my revision in this way:

"Good morning, Moses, I hear that you have some gods in this country. Do you know anything about it?"

"Oh, yes, I'm the head god's head man."

"You are?"

"Yes, I had a talk with the head god—the top one of the three (we are down to three here now), and he told me to tell people what a good god he is, and that they must all praise him up for it."

"He did! Well is that all he said?"

"Oh, no, he told me to tell them that he is the only God, and is the kind father of all, and loves all alike, and that they must all just trust in him and he will take good care of them."

"I thought you said a while ago that there were three of these gods; now this one says he is the only one. Is there trouble in the cabinet?"

"No, there are three, but there is one. See?"

"Well, no, I can't say that I do. But no matter, the rest of that about the father business was pretty good. That was the best I ever heard. But do you know that the very last man I talked with said that this god was partial to some folks and treated some others pretty shabbily."

"Oh, that is not so; my god is no respecter of persons; that's his very strongest hold. He treats rich and poor just alike, only if anything he leans a little toward the poor."

"That is pretty clever. But what else did he tell you in that talk?"

"Well, he told me to tell the people, 'Thou shalt not kill' and afterwards, at another time, he told me to take a lot of my men, and go over there to that town just across, and kill all the men and boys I could find, and if they fought hard for their homes, and I seemed to be getting the worst of it for a little while, not to be afraid, he'd be with me, and he'd see that I came out all right. Oh, he's the gayest old god you ever saw to help in a fight."

"Well, yes, that was pretty clever to you; but isn't he the god of that village too!"

"Oh, yes; but you see one of the men that lives over there went and worshipped another god one day, and this one didn't like it."

"I see; but if he treats them all that way, don't you think it is rather natural that they should go and hunt up another god to admire?"

Well, while I was waiting for Moses to answer this question, I heard another man say that only a day or two previously this very fellow had burned up their homes, and murdered a good many people who had never injured him; and that he had dashed out the brains of the innocent children, and had actually sold the sweet, pure young girls to his brutal soldiers. Since I heard that, my mind has been so occupied with some other little matters that my revision has not gone any farther, and somebody else has got one out; so I don't know that I shall ever finish mine. It does not seem to be very encouraging work any way; and I am afraid that people would find fault with its scholarship if it should be finished.

Theological scholarship and common-sense always did disagree. A man who is well vaccinated with either will never catch the other.

The Church used to keep a box about four feet long and two feet wide which it called the sacred ark of God. It was certain death for any man not a priest to touch that box. It is supposed that they kept in it gold and jewels which they extorted from their dupes, and that for fear of robbery they made superstition their banker. Well, they had to move that jewelry-box once for some reason, and it is not said that anything happened to the men who put it on the cart; but as the man who drove the oxen—in one place it says that they were oxen, in another that they were cows with young calves, and you will be damned if you don't believe both—anyhow, as the driver walked along in horrid fear lest something should happen to that ark of God, the oxen shied, and the ark toppled, and instinctively the driver put out his hand to steady the sacred thing. Well, you would think that any sane man, any reasonable being, would have commended him for it; but no! Jehovah struck him dead for his pains. Why? Because that box was so supremely sacred. Supreme nonsense! Suppose he had not touched it and it had fallen? What then? Most likely Jehovah would then have struck him dead for not touching it. It strikes me that the only reasonable, sensible being connected with that whole story was the driver, the man they abuse, the man the priests murdered, I suspect because he discovered what was in that ark, and threatened to expose the humbug.

Whenever any man uses judgment and common-sense the Church calls him wicked and dangerous. They say he "touches with unholy hands holy things"; and when he dies, whether his death was expedited or otherwise, they say God killed him.

Now, if God did kill that man for touching the ark to save it from falling, what do you think of him—as a God? I can tell you what you would think of him as a man. You would think he was a ruffian and a murderer that is what you would think of him as a man.

Truly gods are made of poor stuff. If I can't have a god that is nobler and better and truer and kinder than the very best man I ever saw, then I don't want any god at all. And candor forbids me to state that I ever saw, heard or read of any such a god. All the gods I ever read or heard of have fallen infinitely below a few men I know.

Jehovah, it seems to me, is hardly an average god, even as gods go. He believed in polygamy. He believed in slavery. He was a murderer—killed 52,000 people once because somebody looked into that four-by-two box that he thought so much of. Human life was not worth a copper in his neighborhood. He was always in a rage about something, and you never knew when he would "get the drop on you" because somebody else had ruffled his temper. "Any man was liable," as the Irishman said, "to wake up any morning and find him-self burned to ashes in his bed," because one of his neighbors had been wicked enough to lend a five-dollar green-back to one of the Philistines, or had eaten a gum-drop in the dark of the moon, or committed some other awful crime like that.

In its day the Bible was all very well, no doubt. It was the expression of the best that the Jewish people then knew in morals. In his time Christ was a great reformer and a brave man. His philosophy was then an onward spring, and he detested the shams of the Church.

But with the knowledge we have to-day we should call that man a lunatic who tried to bind medical science by the teachings of that age, and maintained that when a man was sick he had a devil, and that if he got worse he had a whole flock of them. Yet Christ thought that. We should call the man utterly insane who insisted that Joshua gave us the last light that is ever to be thrown on astronomy. We should simply look with pity on one who should try to convince us that the legal profession ought to be bound by the laws of Moses; and we know that any nation that attempted to act under his guidance would be soon convinced by the unerring voice of foreign cannon that somebody had made a mistake.

Science has grown. Philosophy has developed. International law has sprung up. In religion alone we are asked to accept the standard of morality and honor of ages that are dead—to take as the last word of wisdom the reformer's code of eighteen hundred years ago. We may grow in all else; in this we must stand still. We may use a text-book on Nature, Medicine, Law, or Mechanics, until by its aid we pass beyond its knowledge to a higher; but in morals and religion the book that was a light to the ages of ignorance and superstition, and the production of its brain, must still be the sole illumator of a world made wise and critical and thoughtful by science and deep experience. The fisherman's lantern, although useful in its day, cannot guide us while we stand in the glare of electricity. Why stand persistently with our faces westward, and gaze at the declining light, crying out impotently and hopelessly as we see it grow dim and vanish?

Our wise men have kept steadily onward, guided by the light of the breaking dawn; and with their faces to the East their star has never set. The fishermen's light has sunk below the horizon, leaving behind it the glow of honest labor and earnest effort to keep their memory bright. The scientist's star has risen, and with no claim that it is even yet the highest light—the final promise, it throws its rays of knowledge, its beams of hope, far into the future, and bids us follow, leaving the cold embers of the dead past for the warmth and light of the living future.

The hope of the past is the despair of the future. Stagnation is death. In movement and thought alone is progress. The wealth of the world is the brain of the scholar.

The past is dead; peace to its ashes. The future is ours to form on new models; models deformed by past superstitions, or models though faulty, instinct with true freedom. You are the jury, what is the verdict?

HISTORICAL FACTS AND THEOLOGICAL FICTIONS

It is one of the glittering fictions of the Church that to her civilization is due, and that it is to her benign influence and direction alone that woman has been advanced to her present position in the social scale; that without the Bible and the Church the status of woman in Christian countries would be lower and her lot harder.

1st. To prove this claim she directs attention to the status of woman in several non-Christian countries, and compares the degradation and hardship she there endures to the position of woman to-day in America, England, and France.

2d. The Church claims the credit of originating and sustaining the various steps of progress by which woman has been elevated. She claims to have originated and to sustain the idea that woman is man's equal, and to recognize her as such in the Church.

3d. She points with pride to the superior education and intelligence of the women of Christian countries, and contrasts this intellectual altitude with that of women elsewhere. She says that women owe their superior opportunities of education and advancement to their religion.

4th. But above all the clergy attempt to silence those who ask questions, by calling attention to the superior legal status of woman in Christian countries, and asserting that the Church secured this and that it made marriage honorable and home a possibility.

5th. The clergy claim that the Bible is woman's best friend and staunchest defender, and that it is the originator of morality.

"The moment there is fixation, petrification and death ensue. Profound sincerity is the only basis of character." —Emerson.

We are told that our superior civilization and high moral tone are due to Christianity. I think that this is not true. The whole, or at least much the larger and foundation part of the question of civilization—where it shall grow and where only live, where it shall drag and where scarcely exist—seems to me to be decided primarily by environment, the basis of which is climate and soil.

Where the climate and soil are most favorable to the highest development; where the environment is neither too hard nor too indulgent; where man is neither enervated by heat and the absence of necessity to labor, nor stunted by cold and hardship and the ever-present necessity to search or labor for food and warmth; there will be the highest types and forms of civilization.

If the Buddhist religion had chanced to be the one that in the process of events took root in the climate and soil where the Hebrew Bible and the Christian belief hold sway; and if, on the other hand, the Hebrew and Christian religions had been the ones developed in India or China, the civilization of the various countries would still, in the main, be what they are to-day.

If our superior civilization were the result of our religion, then the most civilized countries would be the most intensely Christian countries. We all know that this is not the case. Compare the intense Christianity of Spain or Russia, and their backward civilization, with the easy-going religious or irreligious condition of France, or America, and their recognition of Liberty and Humanity, equalled nowhere else on earth.

I admit unreservedly that a religion, by its inelasticity, may do much to retard progress, or by its greater elasticity may permit a more rapid development than a more nearly petrified or incoherent system would allow; but what I hold is this, that the primary and controlling causes of the various stages of civilization are climate and soil.

There are, of course, many other things which modify the social development or civilization in any country, as its religion, its laws, and what we may call "accidents of intellectual or civil contest," such as the religions or other wars—our own war in which the blacks were freed, arbitration, and immigration. All of these, and many others, are modifying influences; but no one of them can claim the primary place.

Soil, climate, and location determine the occupation of a nation, as whether it shall be militant, commercial, or agricultural. In turn occupation determines what the character of a people and their laws shall be, whether they shall be warlike or peaceful, inventive or receptive, stationary or roving; and these, in turn, are the matters which determine the civil scale to which a people shall rise.

True, the religion of a people will make itself felt strongly but whenever a nation has found it expedient or desirable to accomplish a feat which was in opposition to its religion, it has invariably modified the religion to fit the case, or waived it in favor of that particular movement.

In keeping with this fact it is found that in those countries where the greatest changes and modifications of government and occupation have occurred, there have the religions undergone the greatest modification to fit the new order of things. If it were the religion that dominated the matter, civilization and morals would be immovable, and legislation would revolve around the guidance of the Church.

According to the very theory of Divine revelation a religion would be most perfect at its beginning. It would be without flaw when born. It would be incapable of improvement or growth. In a word it would be immovable. It would possess the fixation of which Emerson speaks. It would not have to readjust itself to the changed and improved conditions of man, and its word would be always a higher light on every movement of progress. It would be to the Church and not to the State that the great principles of progress, of liberty, and of justice would look for the highest guidance and the last light. How far this is from the real state of things in any country or in any religion all readers of history know.

It is the State or Science which has proposed and made the steps of progress, and the Church has (often after the most bitter fight and denunciation) readjusted her creed to the new code, and then claimed that she had that light and knew that principle before, although neither she nor any one else had ever suspected it.

This has been the case with almost every important discovery that Science has ever made. The Church has retarded the acceptance of the new light and has set her seal of "divine disapproval and damnation" on the brow of the thinkers who strove to bless mankind. It has been the rule in State reforms as well. It was so in the struggle to separate Church and State. It is so in the effort to sustain the belief in the "divine right of kings." The Church fought individual liberty and representative Government, and she still contests the question of individual conscience and individual equality and independence. (NOTE: See reports of the last General Conference of the Methodist Church held in Philadelphia, where, during a heated debate, one member said that he was in favor of using common-sense and the principle of justice in deciding questions of right and wrong and of liberty of conscience; whereupon a large majority voted him a dangerous man, and decided that common-sense and justice had nothing to do with religion. One member naively remarked that the whole career and life of a good preacher fully disproved that any such heretical doctrines obtained in the Church as that the use of common-sense was admissible; and since the majority voted with him it does not seem to be my place to question that fact.)

In these matters the Church has invariably been on the side that ultimately had to go to the wall, and she has become a party to the progress only after the principle has become an established fact.

Now it is the efforts of Science and Law towards the elevation of man and the betterment of his condition in this world—the procuring for him of greater personal advantage, dignity, and liberty—that have marked the progress of civilization.

The climate and soil decided mans occupation; his occupation determined what his higher needs should be; and his higher needs and the gained results of his occupations enabled him to strive for the bettering of his condition and surroundings. The man who lived in a climate favorable to mental and physical activity, and in a country with a rich and varied soil, was enabled to accomplish his ends as his less fortunate brother—lacking such support and stimulus and motive—has been unable to do.

If such a thing had been possible, thirty years ago, as that all knowledge of our religion had been utterly wiped out of America, and a thorough knowledge of Buddhism or Mohammedanism instilled into every Yankee brain in its stead, the Yankee brain would have simply adjusted its religion to its surroundings and not its surroundings to its religion; and America would have gone right on in the front rank of liberty and toleration and progress. There would have been social and political and religious contests over "caste" or "harems" or "Tripitaka," instead of over slavery as a divine institution, the right of a mother to her own offspring, or the inspiration of the Bible. The wheels of progress would have been blocked some days by devotees who preached damnation for those who believed in the "Trinity" instead of for those who did not. Hell would have been as freely promised to the man who suggested that Newton knew more than Mohammed, as it is to-day to any one who makes the same odious comparison between Darwin and Moses. The timid would have been terrified by sermons to prove the lost condition of a man who touched one of lower rank, in place of the edification our clergy often in the shape of eternal damnation for unbaptized infants. And there would have been so little difference between the arguments for the divinity of the Tripitaka and the Bible, and for the miracles of each, that if any devout Presbyterian had by accident left his barrel of sermons on the latter subject behind him, his Buddhist brother could have utilized them without the change of an argument. But the wheel would turn and the devotee would either go down or change his creed, and it would depend chiefly upon his age and consequent flexibility which course he would adopt.

No known religion could transfer the conditions of civilization in China to America or England or France, and no amount of christianizing (if such a thing were possible) could transform China into a like condition with us, so long as her climate, her soil, and her population remain what they are to-day. You may make the Arab or the Jap digest the whole Westminster catechism, but he will, he must, be an Arab or a Jap still—if he lives though it all. If his constitution is good, and he gets over it, his condition and grade of civilization will continue to conform to his environment; and the trifling difference involved, between turning-off prayers on a wheel and counting them off on beads will be simply the difference between tweedledee and tweedledum.

Notwithstanding this as a primary fact, the religion of a country has a modifying influence on the rapidity of its progress, and the more fixed a religion—the more certainly it claims perfection, the greater claim it lays to holding the final word; and the more fully this claim is accepted by the people, the greater influence will it have, the greater check will it be to the development of any new thought, discovery, invention, or principle that arises in the process of evolution toward a freer atmosphere and a broader understanding of individual liberty and dignity and life. William Kingdom Clifford, F.R.S., in his delightful book on the "Scientific Basis of Morals" says:

"It is sometimes said that moral questions have been authoritatively settled by other methods; that we ought to accept this decision, and not to question it by any method of scientific inquiry; and that reason should give way to revelation on such matters.

"I hope before I have done to show just cause why we should pronounce on such teaching as this no light sentence of moral condemnation: first, because it is our duty to form those beliefs which are to guide our actions by the two scientific modes of inference, and by these alone; and, secondly, because the proposed mode of settling ethical questions by authority is contrary to the very nature of right and wrong.

"The worship of a deity who is represented as unfair or unfriendly to any portion of the community is a wrong thing, however great may be the threats and promises by which it is commended. And still worse, the reference of right and wrong to his arbitrary will as a standard, the

diversion of the allegiance of the moral sense from the community to him, is the most insidious and, fatal of social diseases.

"The first principle of natural ethics is the sole and supreme allegiance of conscience to the community.

"Secondly, veracity to the community depends upon faith in man. Surely I ought to be talking platitudes when I say that it is not English to tell a man a lie, or to suggest a lie by your silence or your actions, because you are afraid that he is not prepared for the truth, because you don't quite know what he will do when he knows it, because perhaps after all this lie is a better thing for him than the truth would be, this same man being all the time an honest fellow-citizen whom you have every right to trust. Surely I have headed that this craven crookedness is the object of our national detestation. And yet it is constantly whispered that it would be dangerous to divulge certain truths to the masses. 'I know the whole thing is untrue: but then it is so useful for the people; you don't know what harm you might do by shaking their faith in it.' Crooked ways are none the less crooked because they are meant to deceive great masses of people instead of individuals. If a thing is true, let us all believe it, rich and poor, men, women, and children. If a thing is untrue, let us all disbelieve it, rich and poor, men, women and children. Truth is a thing to be shouted from the housetops, not to be whispered over rose-water after dinner when the ladies go away.

"Even in those whom I would most reverence, who would shrink with horror from such actual deception as I have just mentioned, I find traces of a want of faith in man. Even that noble thinker, to whom we of this generation owe more than I can tell, seemed to say in one of his posthumous essays that in regard to questions of great public importance we, might encourage a hope in excess of the evidence (which would infallibly grow into a belief and defy evidence) if we found that life was made easier by it. As if we should not lose infinitely more by nourishing a tendency to falsehood than we could gain by the delusion of a pleasing fancy. Life must first of all be made straight and true; it may get easier through the help this brings to the commonwealth. And Lange, the great historian of materialism, says that the amount of false belief necessary to morality in a given society is a matter of taste. I cannot believe

that any falsehood whatever is necessary to morality. It cannot be true of my race and yours that to keep ourselves from becoming scoundrels we must needs believe a lie, The sense of right grew up among healthy men and was fixed by the practice of comradeship. It has never had help from phantoms and falsehoods, and it never can want any. By faith in man and piety toward men we have taught each other the right hitherto; with faith in man and piety toward men we shall never more depart from it."

If religion decided and produced the civilization of a people, what sort of civilization would exist to-day among the Jews? All Jews would be bigamists, and murder would be their pastime. No people would be free from their rapine, no woman safe from their lust. But fortunately they have followed their scientific and political leaders instead of their Prophets, and the consequence is that they are so far above and superior to their religion and their Bible, that only in its trivial and immaterial dictates is it their guide and law to-day.

And we, building upon the same foundation, with an added story to our edifice, modify, to suit legislation and a higher public sentiment and a broader conception of justice, both the foundation and the roof whenever a new principle is born or some great soul floods the world with light.

And so the world moves on, those nations in advance that possess the climate to stimulate and the soil to support to the best advantage their citizens—philosophers and scientists who grope towards perfection and stumble on the way over real and imaginary obstacles, but still bring each generation nearer the goal, and freer to brush aside the cobwebs of superstition and ignorance, and to look fairly out on the light that breaks in the East.

There is another feature of the subject that will bear looking at. Christians are the last to give credit to other religions for the development and advance of civilization in the countries possessing them. What Christian will admit that it is the religion of the Chinese that makes them the most orderly, law-abiding, mob-avoiding people on the globe? Will any Christian admit that it is the inferior moral tone of Christ and his teachings which enables the followers of Confucius and Buddha to offer this superior showing? Is he prepared to say that Mohammedanism is superior to Christianity because its followers outdo the Christians in honesty? (Travelers tell us that a native can leave an order together with a bag of uncounted gold at the shop of a dealer, and upon the return of the buyer his order will be exactly filled, his gold properly and honestly divided, and all where he had left them, even though the shop be open to the street and unattended and unguarded.) Is it owing to the superior blessings of the Mormon faith that its followers are more thrifty, and that paupers are few or unknown among them? Is it because their religion is superior to ours that the Lapp women are better treated, that their comparative status is higher, and their family life purer than with ourselves? ("Through Norway with Ladies" By W. Mattieu Williams. F.R.A.S., F.C.S.)

The claim that superiority of civilization is due to Christianity, and that to it we owe the good things of the nations where it is the prevailing religion proves too much. It will work just as well for any other religion as for our own. Its reach is too extended, its conclusion too comprehensive for its purpose. Christianity could not be made its sole terminus. It reminds one of the story of the brakeman who was persuaded to go to church. When he came out his friend asked him how he liked the preacher. He said, "Very well, on the main line. He had good wheels, his track was straight and level, and he carried a good head of steam, but he seems to lack terminal facilities." Horace Seaver recently wrote the following:

It is a very common argument with Christians, that only those nations which have had the Bible were refined, civilized, and learned. A Christian paper, now before us, exultingly says:

"Take the map of the world, draw a line around those, countries that have enjoyed the highest degree of refinement, and you will encircle just those nations that have received the Bible as their authority in religion.

"From this language, the plain inference is, that those nations have been indebted to the influence of the Bible for the positions to which they

have attained. Let us follow out a little this line of argument and see where it will lead.

"The ancient Egyptians stood as far in advance of their contemporaries as do the nations of Christendom at the present day, as the remains of Egyptian cities and temples fully attest. And if the argument is good, they were indebted for that superiority to their worship of cats, crocodiles, and onions!

"The ancient Greek might have exclaimed, as he beheld the proud position to which Greece had attained—'See what we owe to a belief in our glorious mythology; we have reached the highest point of enlightenment the world has ever witnessed; we stand unequalled in power, wealth, the cultivation of the arts, and all that makes a nation refined, polished, and great!'

How immeasurably would his faith in the elevating tendency of his religion have been increased, could he have looked with prophetic eye into the distant ages of the future, and beheld the enlightened and Christianized nations of the nineteenth century adopting the remains of Grecian architecture, sculpture, painting, oratory, music, and literature as their models!

"Pagan Rome, too, once mistress of the world and arbitress of nations—the home of philosophers and sages—the land in which the title, 'I am a Roman citizen,' was the proudest that a mortal could wear—Rome, by the above Christian argument, should have ascribed all her honor, praise, and glory to her mythology.

"The Turk and the Saracen, likewise, have had their day of power and renown. Baghdad was the seat of science and learning at a time when the nations of Europe were sunk in darkness and superstition. The Turk and Saracen should have pointed to the Koran as the source of their refinement.

"Thus we see that for Christian argument we are noticing, if it proves anything, proves too much. If the nations of Christendom are indebted to the Bible for their enlightenment, likewise were the Egyptians indebted to their cat and crocodile, and onion worship, the Greeks and Romans to their mythology, and the Turks and Saracens to their Koran."

It is a fact that in some Christian countries the actual status of woman is higher than it is to-day in any other country; but it is also true that her comparative status is often lower. (See Appendix C, 1-6)

If we compare the actual status of woman in Russia or Spain (the two most intensely Christian countries to-day) with that of the Chinese or Hindoo woman, the showing may be somewhat in favor of the former; but on the other hand, her comparative position (when taken with that of the men of her country) does not gain but loses by the contrast. It is a significant fact that, of all the Christian countries, in those where the Church stands highest and has most power women rank lowest and have fewest rights accorded them, whether of personal liberty or proprietary interest. In the countries named above and in other countries where the Church still has a strong grip upon the throat of the State, woman's position is degraded indeed; while in the three so-called Christian countries where the Church has least power, where law is not wholly or in so large part canonical, woman's position is more free, more independent, and less degraded, when compared with the position of the men of those countries.

That tells the whole story. If it were to the Church or to her religion that she owed her advancement, it would be in the most strictly Christian countries that her elevation and advantages would be greatest. Under the canon law her status would be higher than under the common law. On the contrary, however, it is under the least religious, freest, and most purely secular forms of government that she has attained most full recognition and secured the greatest advancement.

Compare the position of woman in Christian Spain with her position in Infidel France. Compare her condition in Russia, with the flag of the Church and the seal of the Cross for her protection, with that of her sister under the stars and stripes of America, with a constitution written by the infidels Jefferson and Paine.

Compare them and decide whether it is to the Church and the Cross, with their wars and persecutions, or to Liberty and

Skepticism that women owe their loyal love and their earnest support. Compare them and determine then whether it is to Christianity or to Science that she should fly for protection, and where it is that she will be most certain of justice. Compare them and answer whether it is to the Fathers of the Church or to the Founders of Republics that women should be most grateful. Compare them, and be thankful, oh women of America, that the Church never had her hand on the throat of the Constitution of the United States, and that she is losing her grip on the Supreme Bench! (On the status of women there is much of interest in Mr. Herbert Spencer's "Principles of Sociology," vol. 1. Mr. Spencer deals with the subject, in the main, from a different point of view from the one taken in this article; but that his position (in regard to the causes of woman's advancement being due to the Church) is not wholly unlike my own, will, I think, be readily seen. He places more stress on the results of war than I have done (and in this the corroborating evidence furnished by the Holy wars would sustain the position of both), I having included this phase of action under the term occupation, since I have dealt almost wholly with nations more advanced and freer from the fortunes of the Militant type than Mr. Spencer has done.)

In our pride of race we forget that it is less than three hundred short years since Christianity by both legal and spiritual power enforced the most degrading and vile conditions upon woman, compelling her to live solely by the sale of her virtue. (See Appendix D)

Only within the past three hundred years of growing skepticism and loss of power by the Church has either purity or dignity become possible for women; and it is well for us to remember that for over 1500 years of Christianity when the Church had almost absolute power, it never dreamed of elevating woman, or recognizing her as other than an inferior being created solely to minister to the lowest nature of man, and possessing neither a right to her own person nor a voice in her own defence.

I wish that every woman who upholds the Church to-day might read the array of facts on this subject so ably presented by Matilda

Joslyn Gage in her work on "Woman, Church, and State," a digest of which is printed in the last chapter of vol. 1. of the "History of Woman Suffrage," of which she is one of the editors. It is so ably written, and the facts collected are so damning, that I need add no word of mine to such passages as I can give from it, in the accompanying appendix to this work. (See Appendix E.)

Blackstone enumerates three "absolute rights of persons." First, "The right of personal security, in the legal enjoyment of life, limb, body, health, and reputation." Second, "The right of personal liberty—free power of locomotion without legal restraint." Third, "The right of private property—the free use and disposal of his own lawful acquisitions."

None of these three primary and essential rights of persons were conceded to women, and Church law did not rank her as a person deprived of these rights, but held that she was not a person at all, but only a function; therefore she possessed no rights of person in this world and no hope of safety in the next.

As to the first of these "absolute rights of persons," any one of her male relations, or her husband after she passed from one to the other, had absolute power over her, even to the extent of bodily injury, bargain and sale of her person, and death. Nor did even this limit the number of her masters. By both Church and Common Law the lords temporal (barons and other peers) and the Lords spiritual (Archbishops, Bishops, and Abbots) possessed and exercised the right to dispose of her purity, either for a money consideration or as a bribe or present as they saw fit.

(Although England was christianized in the fourth century, it was not until the tenth that a daughter had a right to reject a husband selected for her by her father; and it was not until the same century that a Christian wife of a Christian husband acquired the right of eating at the table with him. For many hundred years the law bound out to servile labor all unmarried women between the ages of eleven and forty.—M.J. Gage.

"Wives in England were bought from the fifth to the eleventh century." (The dates are significant; let the Church respond.)—Herbert Spencer.

"In England, as late as the seventeenth century, husbands of decent station were not ashamed to beat their wives. Gentlemen arranged parties of pleasure for the purpose of seeing wretched women whipped at Bridewell. It was not until 1817 that the public whipping of women was abolished in England."—Spencer. See Appendix E.)

Thus was the forced degradation of woman made a source of revenue to the Church, and a means of crushing her self-respect and destroying her sense of personal responsibility as to her own acts in the matter of chastity, the legitimate outcome of which is to be found in the vast army of women who are named only to be reviled. In them the Church can look on her own work. The fruit is the natural outcome of the training woman received that taught and compelled her always to submit to the dictates of some man, no matter what her own judgment, modesty, or desires might be. She was not supposed to have an opinion or to know right from wrong; and from Paul's injunction, "If you want to know anything ask your husband at home," down to the decisions of the last General Conference of the Methodist Church, the teaching that woman must subordinate her own sense of right and her own judgment to the dictates of someone else—any one else of the opposite sex— from first to last has been as ingenious a method as could have been devised to fill the world with libertines and their victims. (See Appendix F, 2.) It is time for the followers of St. Paul to face the results of their own work.

Under the provisions of the law which held that all "persons" could recover damages for injury—have legal redress for a wrong inflicted upon them—woman again was held as not a person.

If she were assaulted and beaten, or if she were subjected to the greatest indignity that it is possible to inflict upon her, she had no redress. She could not complain. The law gave her no protection whatever. Her father or husband could, if he saw fit, bring suit to recover damages for the loss of her services as a servant, and wholly upon the ground that it was an injury to him and to his feelings. She was no more recognized as a "person" in the matter, nor was she more highly considered than if she were an inmate of a zoological garden to which some mischievous visitor had fed too many bonbons. The owner was damaged because the brute might die or be injured in the sight of the patrons, but aside from that view of the case no harm was done and no account taken of so trivial a matter.

No matter what the injury she sustained, whether it crippled her physically or blighted her mentally and made life to her the worst curse that could be inflicted, she had no appeal. The wounded feelings of one of her male relations received due consideration, and he could recover the money-value he might set upon the injury to his lacerated mind. This is still the letter and the practice of the law in many places, even in America.

If she had no male relations, the injury did not count, and no "person" being injured everything was lovely and prayers went right on to the God who, being no respecter of persons (except they were free, white, adult males), enjoyed the incense from altars whereon burning "witches" writhed in agony and helpless young girls plead for mercy under the loathed and loathsome touch of the "St." Augustine whose praises are chanted and whose divine goodness is recounted by Christendom to-day.

("*To Augustine, whose early life was spent in company with the most degraded of womankind, is Christianity indebted for the full development of the doctrine of Original sin."—Gage.*

"All or at least the greater part of the fathers of the Greek Church before Augustine, denied any real original sin."—Emerson.

"The doctrine had a gradual growth, and was fully developed by Augustine."—Waite, and *"St." Pelayos, ("The abbot elect of St. Augustine, at Canterbury, in 1171, was found on investigation to have seventeen illegitimate children in a single village. An abbot of St. Pelayo in Spain, in 1130, was proved to have kept no less than seventy mistresses. Henry III., Bishop of Liege, was deposed in 1274 for having sixty-five illegitimate children."—Lecky, "History of European Morals."*

"This same bishop boasted, at a public banquet, that in twenty-two months fourteen children had been born to him. A license to the

clergy to keep concubines was during several centuries levied by princes."—Ibid.)

"It was openly attested that 100,000 women in England alone were made dissolute by the clergy."—Draper, "Intellectual Development of Europe.")

Such was the "elevation" and civilization offered by the Church to woman. These are among her debts to the Church, and the men who fought and contended against the incorporation of such infamy into the common law were branded as infidels. It was said they denied their Lord. They were pronounced most dangerous, and the clergy held up their hands in holy horror and whispered that such men "as much as denied the Bible, blasphemed their God, and sold their souls to the Devil." And the women, poor dupes, believed it.

One method the Church took to benefit woman and show its respect for her was this: any married man was prohibited from being a priest. Women were so unholy, so unclean, and so inferior, that to have one as a wife degraded a man to such an extent that he was unfit to be a minister or to touch holy things. The Catholic Church still prohibits either party who is so unholy as to marry from profaning its pulpit; but the Protestant Churches divide up, giving women the disabilities and men the offices. The unselfishness of such a course is quite touching. It says to women "you support us and we will damn you; there is nothing mean about us."

As to Blackstone's second count—"the right to personal liberty"—I can perhaps do no better than give a few bald facts.

Under Pagan rule the personal liberty of woman had become very considerable, as well as her proprietary liberty; but Christianity began her degradation at once.

Christianity was introduced into England in the fourth century, and the sale of women began in the fifth; and it was not until the eleventh that a girl could refuse to marry any suitor her father chose for her. In a word, she always had a guardian; she had no personal liberty whatever; she could neither buy nor own property as her brothers could; she could not marry when and whom she preferred, live where she wished, eat, drink, or wear what she liked, or refuse any of these provisions when they were offered by her male relatives. If they decided that she had too many back teeth they simply pulled them out, and she had nothing to say on the subject. She could be sold outright by her father, or leased or bound out as he preferred. She never got so old but that her earnings belonged to him, and a mother never arrived at an age sufficiently advanced to be entitled to the earnings of her children.

Sharswood says, "A father is entitled to the benefits of his children's labor." "An infant (any one not of age) owes reverence and respect to his mother; but she has no right to his services." (Blackstone, Sharswood.)

This is upon the theory, doubtless, that starvation is wholesome for a widowed mother, but that it does not agree with a father's digestion at any time.

Sir Henry Maine in his "Ancient Law" says, that from the Pagan laws all this inequality and oppressiveness of guardianship and restriction of the personal liberty of women had disappeared, and he adds: "The consequence was that the situation of the Roman female, whether married or unmarried, became one of great personal and proprietary independence. But Christianity tended somewhat from the very first to narrow this remarkable liberty . . . . The great jurisconsult himself (Gaius) scouts the popular Christian apology offered for it in the mental inferiority of the female sex . . . . Led by their theory of Natural Law, the Roman (Pagan) jurisconsult had evidently at this time assumed the equality of the sexes as a principle of their code of equity."

Of the Christians, led by their theory of a revealed divine law which treated women as inferior beings and useful only as prey, Lecky says ("European Morals," vol. 1, page 358): "But in the whole feudal (Christian and chiefly Canon) legislation women were placed in a much lower legal position than in the Pagan empire. The complete inferiority of the sex was continually maintained by the law; and that generous public opinion which in Pagan Rome had frequently revolted against the injustice done to girls, in depriving them of the greater part of the inheritance of their fathers, totally disappeared. Wherever the canon law had been the basis of legislation, we find laws of succession sacrificing the interest of daughters and of wives, and a state of public opinion which has been formed and regulated by these laws; nor was any serious attempt made to abolish them till the close of the last century. The French revolutionists, though rejecting the proposal of Sieyes and Condorcet (both infidels) to accord political emancipation to women, established at least an equal succession of sons and daughters, and thus initiated a great reformation of both law and opinion which sooner or later must traverse the world."

How soon or how late this will happen will depend very greatly upon the amount of power retained by the Church. Pagans, Infidels, and Scientists have fought for, and the Church has fought against, the dignity, honor, and welfare of women for centuries; and because fear, organization, wealth, selfishness, and power have been on the side of the Church, and she has kept women too ignorant to understand the situation, she has succeeded for many generations in retarding the progress and shutting out the light that slowly came in despite of her.

"No society which preserves any tincture of Christian institutions is ever likely to restore to married women the personal liberty conferred on them by the middle Roman law; but the proprietary disabilities of married females stand on quite a different basis from their personal incapacities, and it is by keeping alive and consolidating the former that the canon law has so deeply injured civilization. There are many vestiges of a struggle between the secular and ecclesiastical principles; but the canon law nearly everywhere prevailed." (Maine's "Ancient Law," 158.)

It has always been uphill work fighting the Church. So long as it had sword and fagot at its command, and the will to use them; so long as it pretended to have, and people believed that it had, power to mete out damnation to its appeasers; just so long were science, justice, and thought fatally crippled.

But when Voltaire, Diderot, Condorcet and the great encyclopedist circle of France got their hands on the throat of the

Church, and dipped their pens in the fire of eloquence, wit, ridicule, reason, and justice, then, and not till then, began to dawn a day of honor toward women, of humanity and justice, and truth. They drew back the curtain, the world saw, the cloud lifted, and life began on a new plane. Under Pagan rule woman had begun, as we have seen, to receive recognition apart from sex. She was a human being. A general law of "persons" applied to and shielded her. But from the first the Christian Church refused to consider her apart from her capacity for reproduction; and this one ground of consideration it pronounced a curse, a crime, and a shame to her. (See Lea's "Sacerdotal Celibacy.") Her only claim to recognition at all was a curse. She was not a person, she was only a function.

Man it pronounced a person first, with rights, privileges, and protection as such. Incidentally he might also be a husband, a father, or a son. His welfare, duties, and rights as a person, as a human being, were apart from and superior to those that were special and incidental. He received consideration always as a person. He might be dealt with as husband or father.

But ignoring all her mental life and denying that she had any, and ignoring all her physical possibilities, ambitions, desires, and capabilities as a person, the Church narrowed woman's life and restricted her energies into a compass where its power over her became absolute and her subjection certain. Nor has the loss been wholly to woman, for any influence which cripples the mother's capacity of endowment takes cruel revenge on the race. ("It is not impossible but that a more correct understanding of the laws of life and heredity may establish the fact that because of the subjection of woman, the entire race has been mentally dwarfed and physically weakened."—Gamble.)

From this outlook the debt of civilization to the Church is heavy indeed. Is it a debt of gratitude?

Under this head there is space for but one point farther, out of the great store at hand. The clergy were licensed to commit crime. They got up a neat little scheme called "benefit of clergy" by which they were secure from the punishment meted out to other criminals. The relief offered did sometimes reach other men, but as learning was largely confined to the clergy they were the chief beneficiaries, as the name implies and as was the intent of the law. Any man who could read was allowed "benefit of clergy"; in other words, his punishment was lightened or entirely omitted. But a woman, though she were a perfect mine of wisdom and could read in any number of languages, could receive no such benefit, because she could not take holy orders. They first enacted that she should not take orders, and then they denied to her the relief which only that ability could give. So great a favorite was woman with the Church!

The ordinary male criminal received the ordinary punishment. The clergy received none; and in order that the requisite gross amount of suffering for crime should be inflicted on somebody, the clergy enacted that woman should receive their share vicariously in addition to her own, and then to this they added such interest as would make the twenty-per-cent-a-month men of Wall Street ashamed of their stupid financiering.

Thus the Church arrogated to itself the exclusive right to commit crime with impunity, and also claimed and exercised the right to prevent women from learning to read. If she still persisted it could then punish her doubly, because she had no right to learn.

For offenses for which ordinary men were hanged, women were burned alive, and priests were glorified. For larceny a man was branded in the hand or imprisoned for a few months while for a first offence of the kind a woman was kindly permitted to be hanged or beheaded without benefit of clergy; and the clergy went scot free. (Blackstone, Christian.) The Church did then as it does now, it claimed all the benefits of citizenship and paid none of the penalties and bore none of the burdens. (It still claims exemption from taxation, thus throwing its burden on others; and it also claims immunity from the very gambling laws which it so rigidly enforces against other institutions.)

The Church did then just as it does now, in principle, in setting up certain great benefits which only priests might hope to obtain, and then enacting that certain persons were forever ineligible to the priesthood; and the same or quite as good reasons were given for denying women such relief from the penalties of the law as was freely extended to men, as are given to-day for refusing her the liberty, emoluments, and benefits that are freely accorded to the most imbecile little theological student who is educated by the needle of a sister and supported by money wrung from the fears of shop or factory girls, to whom he paints the terrors of hell, and freely threatens the same to those who disobey him. Salvation comes high, but no preacher ever gets so poor that he cannot distribute hell free of charge to the multitude without the least diminution of his stock-in-trade.

I should think that an orthodox pulpit would be about the last place a self-respecting woman would wish to fill; but I am glad, since there are some who do so wish, that the issue has again been forced upon the Church, and that in 1884, true to her history, she was again compelled to acknowledge herself a respecter of persons, a degrader of women, and a clog to progress and individual liberty, equality, and conscience.

I am glad that women have recently forced the Methodist and Presbyterian Churches to declare their principles of class preference and partial legislation. I am glad that in 1884 these Churches were compelled to say in effect to women, so that the world could hear: "You are not and you never can be our equals. We are holy. You are unclean. We will hold you back and down to the ancient level we made for you just as long as the life is in us; and if you ever receive recognition as a human being, it must be at the hands of those who defy the Church and hate creeds that are not big enough to go all round. Our creeds are only large enough to give each sex half. But we won't be stingy, we only want our share. You are entirely welcome to all the degradation here and all the damnation hereafter; and any man who attempts to deprive you of these blessings is a heretic and a sinner. Let us pray."

In dealing with this point the humor of the situation is too plain to require comment, and I need only cite a few facts in order to place the beautiful little fiction where it belongs. (See Appendix T.)

As to general education it is well known that the Church has fought investigation and persecuted science. From the third century to Bruno, and from Bruno to Darwin and Tyndall there is an unbroken chain of evidence as to her position in these matters and her opposition to the diffusion of knowledge. When, however, it became impossible for her to resist the demand of the people for education; when she could no longer retard liberty and prevent the recognition of individual rights; then she modestly demanded the right to do the teaching herself and to control its extent and scope. (See Appendix G, 1-4.)

With a brain stultified by faith (See Appendix U.) She proposed to regulate investigations in which the habit of faith would necessarily prove fatal to the discovery of truth. (See Clifford's "Scientific Basis of Morals," pp. 25-6.) She proposed to teach nothing but the dead languages and theology, and to confine knowledge to these fields, and she succeeded for many generations in so doing. Every time she found a man who had discovered something, or who had a theory he was trying to test by some little scientific investigations, she cried "heretic" and suppressed that man. She stuck to the dead languages, and the only thing she is not afraid of to-day is something dead. Any other kind of knowledge is a dangerous acquaintance for her to make. (See Morley's "Diderot," p. 190.)

If you meet a clergyman to-day who has devoted his time to the dead languages you need not be afraid that he is a heretic; but if he is studying the sciences, arts, literature, and history of the living world in earnest you can get your fagot ready. His orthodoxy is a dead doxy. It is only a question of time and bravery when he will swear off. (See Ibid, p. 126.)

In the Church schools and "universities" to-day it is quite pathetic to hear the professors wrestle with geology and Genesis, and cut their astronomy to fit Joshua. If in one of these institutions for the petrifaction of the human mind there is a teacher who is either not nimble enough to escape the conclusions of a bright pupil or too honest to try, he is at once found to be "incompetent as an instructor," and is dropped from the faculty. I know one case where it took twenty years to discover that a professor was not able to teach geology—and it took a heresy-hunter with a Bible to do it then.

But it is the claim of the Church in regard to the education of women with which I have to do here.

Women in Greece and Rome under Pagan rule had become learned and influential to an unparalleled degree. (See Lecky, Milman, Diderot, Morley, Christian, and others.)

The early Fathers of the Church found women thirsty for knowledge and eager for opportunities to learn. They there-upon set about making it disreputable for a woman to know anything, ("In the fourth century we find that holy men in council gravely argued the question, and that too with abundant confidence in their ability and power to decide the whole matter: 'Ought women to be called human beings?' A wise and pious father in the Church, after deliberating solemnly and long on the vexed question of women, finally concluded: 'The female sex is not a fault in itself, but a fact in nature for which women themselves are not to blame;' but he graciously cherished the opinion that women will be permitted to rise as men, at the resurrection. A few centuries later the masculine mind underwent great agitation over the question: 'Would it be consistent with the duties and uses of women for them to learn the alphabet?' And in America, after Bridget Gaffort had donated the first plot of ground for a public school, girls were still denied the advantages of such schools. The questions—'Shall women be allowed to enter colleges?' and 'Shall they be admitted into the professions?' have been as hotly contested as has been the question of their humanity."—Gamble.) and in order to clinch their prohibition the Church asserted that women was unable to learn, had not the mental capacity, ("There existed at the same time in this celebrated city a class of women, the glory of whose intellectual brilliancy still survives; and when Alcibiades drew around him the first philosophers and statesmen of Greece, 'it was a virtue to applaud Aspasia;' of whom it has been said that she lectured publicly on rhetoric and philosophy with such ability that Socrates and Alcibiades gathered wisdom from her lips, and so marked was her genius for statesmanship that Pericles afterward married her and allowed her to govern Athens, then at the height of its glory and power. 'Numerous examples might be cited in which Athenian women rendered material aid to the state.'"— Gamble.) was created without mental power and for purely physical purposes. It was maintained that her "Sphere" was clearly defined, and that it was purely and solely an animal one; and worst of all it was stoutly asserted that her greatest crime had always been a desire for wisdom, and that it was this desire which brought the penalty of labor and death into this world. (See Morley's "Diderot," p. 76; Lea's "Sacerdotal Celibacy:" Lecky's "European Morals.")

With such a belief it is hardly strange that the education of girls was looked upon as a crime; and with such a record it is almost incredible effrontery that enables the Church to-day to claim credit for the education of women. (See Appendix H, 1 to 4.) If she were to educate every woman living, free of charge, in every branch of known knowledge, she could not repay woman for what she has deprived her of in the past, or efface the indignity she has already offered. (Lecky, "European Morals," p. 310.)

A prominent clergyman of the Church of England, who was recently much honored in this country, lately said; in a sermon to women: "There are those who think a woman can be taught logic. This is a mistake. Men are logical, women are not." He was too modest to give his proofs. It seemed to me strange that he did not mention the doctrines of the trinity and vicarious atonement, or a few of the miracles, as the result of logic in the masculine mind. And I could not help thinking at the time that a man whose mental furniture was chiefly composed of the thirty-nine articles and the Westminster Catechism would naturally be a profound authority on logic. An orthodox preacher talking about logic is a sight to arouse the compassion of a demon. Next to the natural sciences, logic can give the Church the colic quicker than any other kind of a green apple. And so it is not strange that the clergy should be afraid that it would disagree with the more delicate constitution of a woman. They always did maintain that any diet that was a trifle too heavy for them couldn't be digested by anybody else; and they would be perfectly right in their supposition if intellectual dyspepsia or softening of the brain were contagious.

The "sphere" of no other creature is wholly determined and bounded by one physical characteristic or capacity. To every other creature is conceded without question the right to use more than one talent.

But the Fathers decided in holy and solemn council that it would be "unbecoming" for a woman to learn the alphabet, and that she could have no possible use for such information. They said that she would be a better mother without distracting her dear little brain with the a, b, c's, and that therefore she should not learn them. They also decided that she who was so far lost to modesty as to become acquainted with the multiplication table "was an unfit associate for our wives and mothers." There was something wrong with such a woman. She was either a "witch" or else she was "married to the devil."

That is the way the Church encouraged education for women. This was done, the holy Fathers said, to "protect women from the awful temptations of life to which the Lord in his infinite wisdom had subjected man." They had too much respect for their wives and mothers to permit them to come in contact with the wickedness of long division or cube root, and they hoped while life lasted that no man would be so negligent of duty as to allow his sister to soil her pure mind with conic sections.

Well, in time there were a few women brave enough, and a few men honorable and moral enough, to set aside the letter of this prohibition; but much of its spirit still blossoms in all its splendor in Columbia, Harvard, Yale, and various other institutions of learning, where women are either not permitted to enter at all or are required to learn and accomplish unaided that which it takes a large faculty of instructors and every known or obtainable educational device (together with future business stimulus) to enable the young men to do the same thing!

The Fathers said, in effect, "It was through woman wanting to know something that sin came into this world; therefore let her hereafter want to know nothing." They taught that a desire for knowledge on the part of woman was the greatest crime ever committed on this earth, and that it so enraged God that he punished it by death and by every curse known to man. When it was pointed out that animals had lived and died on this earth long before man could have lived, they said that God knew Adam was going to live and Eve was going to sin, so he made death retroactive because Adam would represent all animals when he should be created!

All this was thought and done and taught in order to agree with the silly story of the "fall of man in the Garden of Eden," which every one acquainted with the simple rudiments of science or the history of the races knows to be a childish legend of an undeveloped people. Instead of a "fall" from perfect beginnings, there has been and is a constant rise in the moral as well as in the mental and physical conditions of man. The type is higher, the race nobler and nearer perfection than it ever was before; and the stories of our Bible are the same as those of all other Bibles, simply the effort of ignorant or imaginative men to account for the origin and destiny of things of which they had no accurate knowledge. (One of the Simplest and most interesting explanations of this latter point will be found in "The Childhood of Religions," by Edward Clodd, F.R.A.S., where the Christian reader may be surprised to find that the "ten-commandment" idea (with a number of them which apply to general morals, as "Thou shalt not kill," etc.) is not confined to our Bible, but is found also in the Buddhist Bible in the same form; that the "golden rule" was given by Confucius 500 years before Christ; and that Christianity, when taken as it should be with the other great religions and examined in the same way, presents no problem, no claim, and no proofs which are not found in equal strength in one or more of the other forms of faith. In the matters of morality, miracles, and power to attract and "comfort" multitudes of people, it ranks neither first nor last. It is simply one of several, and in no essential matter is it different from them.)

St. Paul said, "If they (women) will learn anything, let them ask their husbands at home"; and the colossal ignorance of most women would seem to indicate that they have obeyed the command to the letter. But fortunately for women the civilization of freedom has outgrown St. Paul as it has the dictates of the Church, and one by one the doors of information, and hence the doors to honest labor, have been opened, and the possibility of living with dignity and honor has replaced the forced degradation of the days when the power of the Church enabled it to reduce woman to the animal existence it so long forced upon her.

So long as the Church allowed woman but one avenue of support, so long did it force her to use that single means of livelihood. So long as it made her believe that she could bring to this world nothing of value but her capacity to minister to the lower animal wants of man, so long did it force upon her that single alternative—or starvation.

So long as it is able to make multitudes of women believe themselves of value for but one purpose, just that long will it continue to insure the degradation of many of those women who are helpless, or weak, or loving, or ignorant of the motives of those in whose power they are. So long as it teaches woman that she can repay her debt to the world in but one way, so long will it promote commerce in vice and revenue in shame.

Every man is taught that he can repay his debt to this world in many ways. He has open to him many avenues of happiness, many paths to honorable employment. If he fails in one there is still hope. If he misses supreme happiness in marriage he has still left ambition, labor, study, fame; if the one failure overtakes him, no matter how sad, he still can turn aside and find, if not joy, at least occupation and rest.

But the Church has always taught woman that there is but one "sphere," one hope, one occupation, one life for her. If she fails in that, what wonder that with broken hope comes broken virtue or despair? Every woman who has fallen or lost her way has been previously taught by the Church that She had and has but one resource; that there is open to her in life but one path; that whether that path be legally crooked or straight, she was created for but one purpose; that man is to decide for her what that purpose is; and that she must under no circumstances set her own judgement up against his.

The legitimate fruits of such an education are too horribly apparent to need explanation. Every fallen woman is a perpetual monument to the infamy of a religion and a social custom that narrow her life to the possibilities of but one function, and provide her no escape—a system that trains her to depend wholly on one physical characteristic of her being, and to neglect all else.

That system teaches her that her mind is to be of but slight use to her; that her hands may not learn the cunning of a trade nor her brain the bearings of a profession; that mentally she is nothing; and that physically she is worse than nothing only in so far as she may minister to one appetite. I hold that the most legitimate outcome of such an education is to be found in the class that makes merchandise of all that woman is taught that she possesses that is of worth to herself or to this world. No system could be more perfectly devised to accomplish this purpose. (See Lea's II Sacerdotal Celibacy.)

We are told that women owe honorable marriage to Christianity: (See Appendix I, 1-2.) that the more beautiful and tender relations of husband and wife find their root there; that Christianity protects and elevates the mother as no other law or religion ever has.

Let us see. On this subject I find in Maine's "Ancient Law" these facts:

"*Although women had been objects of barter and sale, according to barbaric usages, between their male relatives, the later Roman (Pagan)*

law having assumed, on the theory of Natural Law, the equality of the
sexes, control of the person of women was quite obsolete when Chris-
tianity was born. Her situation had become one of great personal lib-
erty and proprietary independence, even when married, and the arbi-
trary power over her of her male relations, or her guardian, was reduced
to a nullity, while the form of marriage conferred on the husband no
superiority."

Thus as a daughter and as a wife had she grown to be honored
and recognized as an equal under Pagan rule.

"But Christianity tended from the first to narrow this remarkable
liberty . . . . The latest Roman (Pagan) law, so far as touched by the
constitutions of the Christian emperors, bears marks of reaction against
these great liberal doctrines."—Maine.

And again began the sale of women. Christianity held her as
unclean and in all respects inferior; and "during the era which
begins modern history the woman of dominant races are seen everywhere under various forms of archaic guardianship, and the
husband pays a money price to her male relations for her. The
prevalent state of religious sentiment may explain why it is that
modern jurisprudence has absorbed among its rudiments much
more than usual of those rules (archaic) concerning the position of
women which belong peculiarly to an imperfect civilization."—
Ibid.

Thus it will be seen that from the first, and extending down to
the present, the Church did all she could to cast woman back into
the night of the race from which in a great measure she had been
rescued through the ages when Natural Law and not "revelation"
was the guide of man. The laws which the Church found liberal
and just toward women it discarded, and it searched back in the
ages of night for such as it saw fit to re-enact for her. Of this Maine
says: "The husband now draws to himself the power which for-
merly belonged to his wife's male relatives, the only difference
being that he no longer pays anything for the privilege."

As Christians grew economical wives came cheaper than for-
merly, and it became a dogma that wives were not worth much

anyhow, and then, too, it enabled persons of limited means to have more of them. Of a somewhat later date Maine says: "At this point heavy disabilities begin to be imposed upon wives."

That was to make marriage honorable and attractive, no doubt, and, says Maine: "It was very long before the subordination entailed on women by marriage was sensibly diminished." And what diminution it received came from men who fought against Church law. (See Lecky, Maine, Lea, Milman, Christian, Blackstone, Morley, and others for ample proof of this fact.)

It was only the crumbs of liberty, honor, and justice extorted by men who fought the Church on behalf of wives that lightened their most oppressive burdens. It was true then, and it is true to-day, that women owe what justice and freedom and power they possess to the fact that the best and clearest-headed men are more honorable than our religion, and that they have invited Moses and St. Paul to take a back seat. Moses has complied, and St. Paul is half-way down the aisle.

Some of the clergy now explain that although Paul may have written certain things inimical to women, he did not mean them, so it is all right. Such passages as 1 Cor. xi. 3-9; xiv. 34-35; and Eph, v, 22-24, are now explained to be intended in a purely Pickwickian sense; and a Rev. Mr. Boyd, of St. Louis, has even gone so far as to produce the doughty apostle before a woman-suffrage society, as on their side of that argument. This second conversion of St. Paul impresses one as even more remarkable than his first. It took an "angel of God" to show him the error of his ways in Ephesus, but one little Baptist preacher did it this time— all by himself. Truly St. Paul is getting easier to deal with than he use to be.

But to resume, Maine, in tracing the amalgamation of the later Roman (pagan) law with the archaic laws of a lower civiliza-tion (the result of which was Christian law), shows that the Church, while it chose the Roman laws, which had arrived at so high a state, for others, retained for women, and particularly for wives, the least favorable of the Roman, eked out with the archaic Patria

Potestas and the more degrading provisions of the earlier civilizations. Maine reluctantly says that the jurisconsult of the day contended for better laws for wives, but that the Church prevailed in most instances, and established the more oppressive ones.

With certain of these laws—the worst ones—I cannot deal here for obvious reasons; but a few of them I may be permitted to give without offence to the modesty of any one.

Blackstone says "By marriage the husband and wife are one person in law; that is, the very being or legal existence of the woman is suspended during the marriage, or at least is incorporated and consolidated into that of the husband. The husband becomes her baron or lord—she his servant. Upon this principle of the union of person in husband and wife depend almost all the legal rights, duties, and disabilities they acquire by marriage."

That is to say the husband acquires all the rights, and the wife all the disabilities; and the Church wishing to be fair has made the latter as many as possible.

"And therefore," continues Blackstone, "it is also generally true, that all compacts made between husband and wife, when single, are voided by the intermarriage." The working of this principle has been so often illustrated as to render comment unnecessary. A wife retains no rights which her husband is bound to respect, no matter how solemn the compact before marriage, nor what her belief in its strength might have been.

Fortunately for women, happily for wives, men are more decent than their religion; and the law of custom and public opinion has largely outgrown this enactment of the Church, made when she had the power to thus degrade women and brutalize men.

"If the wife be injured in her person or her property she can briny no action for redress without her husband's concurrence and in his name," and on the basis of loss of her services to him as a servant. *"But in criminal prosecutions, it is true, the wife may be indicted and punished separately." (Blackstone.)*

In the case of punishment the Church was entirely willing to give the devil his due. It had no ambition to deprive women of any indictments and punishments that were to be had. In this case, although the husband and wife were one, she was that one. Where privileges or property-rights were to be considered, he was the "one." Such grand reversible doctrines were always on tap with the clergy, and their barrel was always full. Truly, wives do owe much to the Church.

Some of the provisions of these laws have, of late years, been modified by the efforts of men who were pronounced "infidels, destroyers of the Bible, the home, and the dignity of women," aided by women whom the orthodox deride as "strong-minded, ill-balanced, coarse, impious," etc., etc., ad infinitum, ad nauseam. A strong mind, whether in man or woman, has always been to the clergy as a red rag to a bull.

"A woman may make a will, with the assent of her husband, by way of appointment of her personal property. She cannot even with his consent devise lands . . . . Although our law in general considers a man and wife as one person, yet there are some instances where she is considered separately as his inferior," (Ibid.) and for that trip only. As I remarked before when it comes to penalties she is welcome to the whole lot.

"She may not make a deed."

"A man may administer moderate correction to his wife."

"These are the chief legal effects of marriage. Even the disabilities of the wife," Blackstone naively remarks, "are for the most part intended for her protection; so great a favorite is the female sex of the laws of England!"

I should think that if this latter point were not quite clear to a woman, "moderate correction" might convince her that she was quite an unreasonable favorite—beyond her most eager desires. Where the Pagan law recognized her as the equal of her husband, the Church discarded that law, and based the Canon Law upon an archaic invention.

Where Maine speaks of the later growth of Pagan law and of Christian influence upon it, he says: "But the chapter of law relating to married women was for the most part read by the light, not of Roman (or Pagan) but of Canon (or Church) Law, which in no one particular departs so widely from the (improved) spirit of the secular jurisprudence as in the view it takes of the relations created by marriage. This was in part inevitable, since no society which possesses any tincture of Christian institutions is likely to restore to married women the personal liberty conferred on them by the middle Roman law."

Women who support the clergy with one hand, and hold out the other for the ballot; who one day express indignation at the refusal to them of human recognition, and the next day intone the creeds, will have to learn that there is nothing which has so successfully stood, and still so powerfully stands, in the way of the individual liberty, human rights, and dignity of wives, as the Church which they support.

Blackstone says: "In times of popery a great variety of impediments to marriage were made, which impediments might, however, be bought off with money."

You could, for instance, bay a more distant relationship to your future wife for so much cash down to the Church. If your inamorata were your first cousin, you could remove her several degrees with five hundred dollars, and make her no relation at all for a little more. Such little sleight-of-hand performances are as nothing to a well-trained clergyman. Slip a check into one hand, and a request to marry your aunt into the other, let a clergyman shake them up in the coffers of the Church, and when one comes out gold, the other will appear as a blushing bride not even related to her own father, and not more than third cousin to herself.

Of the claim made by the early Christian Fathers, that it was because of the mental inferiority and incapacity of women that the more unjust and binding laws were enacted for them, thus doing all they could to create and intensify by law the incapacity with which they asserted was imposed by God, Maine says: "But the proprietary disabilities of married females stand on quite a different basis from personal incapacity, and it is by the tendency of their doctrines to keep alive and consolidate the former, that the expositors of the Canon Law have deeply injured civilization."

He adds that there are many evidences of a struggle between secular principles in favor of justice for wives, and ecclesiastical principles against it, "but the Canon Law nearly everywhere prevailed. The systems which are least indulgent to married women are invariably those which have followed the Canon Law exclusively . . . . It enforced the complete legal subjection of wives."

Lecky says Fierce invectives against the sex form a conspicuous and grotesque portion of the writings of the Fathers. Woman was represented as the door of hell, as the mother of all human ills. She should be ashamed at the very thought that she is a woman . . . . Women were even forbidden, in the sixth century, on account of their impurity, to receive the Eucharist into their naked hands. Their essentially subordinate position was continually maintained. This teaching in part determined the principles of legislation concerning the sex. (See Appendix J.) The Pagan laws during the empire had been continually repealing the old disabilities of women, and the legislative movement in their favor continued with unabated force from Constantine to Justinian, and appeared also in some of the early laws of the barbarians. But in the whole feudal (Christian) legislation women were placed in a much lower legal position than in the Pagan empire.

And he adds that the French revolutionists (the infidel party) established better laws for women, "and initiated a great reformation of both law and opinion, which sooner or later must traverse the world." And these reformations, being in Christendom will be calmly claimed in the future, as in the present, as due to the beneficent influence of the Church. The Church always belongs to the conservative party, but after a good thing is established in spite of her, she says: "Just see what I have done! 'See what a good boy am I!'"

Not many years ago a few great-souled men who were, "heretics" got a glimpse of a principle which has electrified the world. They said that individual liberty is a universal right; they maintained that humanity is a unit, with interests and aims indivisible, and that liberty to use to the utmost advantage all natural abilities cannot be denied one-half of the race without crippling both. A few even went so far as to suggest that the assumption of the inferiority of women, and the imposition of disabilities upon them, under the claim of divine authority, is the greatest crime in the great calendar of crime for which the Church has yet to render a reckoning to humanity.

To one who reads the history of Canon Law, it is not strange that Christian Judges still decide that women are "incompetent to practice law," and that they should not be allowed to study it. A woman well versed in the history of ancient and modern law might easily be an uncomfortable advocate for such a judge to face. He would probably feel the need of an umbrella.

It is not strange that Columbia College, with its corps of clergymen, "fails to see the propriety" of opening its doors to women. The few clergymen who have for some little time past taken the side of fair-play in this and like matters have simply deserted their colors and come over to the side they are worldly-wise enough to see is to be the side of the future. When it comes to diplomacy the Church is always on deck in time to gather in the spoils; but she stays safely below during the engagement, and simply holds back and anchors firm until she sees which way it is likely to end.

The moment there is an understanding on the part of women of what they owe to Church Law, that moment will end educational clerical monopolists, such as the champion anchor of Columbia, be compelled to earn an honest living in some honest business pertaining to this world. It will be a great day for women when they refuse to longer support these pretenders to divine knowledge, who are willing, at so much a head, to tell what they do not know at the expense of the pale, tired needle-woman, who is in want of almost every comfort that money can buy in this world, together with the surplus gold of the fashionable devotees who minister to the vanity of the clergy, and give to the coffers of the Church that which would save thousands of young girls from degradation and crime, and put the roses of health on the cheek of innocence.

Every dollar that is paid to support the Church is paid to degrade a woman. Every collection that is made to spread "revelation" is used to suppress enlightenment and retard civilization. Every dollar that is invested in "another world" is a dollar diverted from useful purposes in this. Every hour that is spent mooning about "heaven" is that much time taken from needed labor here.

If our energies were wanted in another world we should most likely be in another world. Since we are in this one it is a pretty strong hint that we are expected to attend to business right here. We can't do justice to two worlds at the same time: and since we are assured that we shall have the whole of eternity to arrange matters in the next one, it leaves very little time by comparison to devote to our duties in this.

There we are to have nothing to do but sing and be happy—twang a harp and smile.

Here we have pain to alleviate, ignorance to dispel, innocence to protect, disease to master, and crime to restrain and prevent. Here we have the helpless to shield and guard and protect. Here we have homes to make happy, the hearts of husbands and wives to make glad, the light of love and trust to kindle in the eyes of children. Here is old age to cheer and console. Here are orphans to educate and protect, widows to comfort, and oppression to uproot.

There—nothing to do but look after yourself and manage your harp; nobody to help—all will be perfect; nothing to learn—all will be wise; no hearts to cheer—all will be happy. All that a mother will have to do if she gets a little tired practicing on her lyre and feels gloomy will be to just take a good look over the wall, and photograph on her eyes the picture of her husband and children freshly dipped in oil and put on the griddle, and she will come back to business perfectly satisfied, take up her song where she left off, and praise the Lamb for his infinite mercy. All eternity to learn how to fly round in a robe and keep time with the orchestra! Why a deaf man could learn to do that in fifty or sixty years, and then have all the rest of the time to spare.

We are here such a little while, there is so much to learn, there is so much to do, there is so much to undo, that no man can afford to waste his time on an infinite future of time, space, and leisure. Men cannot afford to lose your best energies. "God" can get on very well without them. Time is short, and needs are pressing; and this thing you know—you can keep busy doing good right here. If there is a hereafter, could there be a better preparation for it than that?

After all that has preceded this page I need hardly do more with this count of the last claim of "Theological Fiction" than simply say, if the Bible is woman's best friend, then the clergy, without authority and in violation of the precepts of their own guide, have been her worst enemy, either through malice or ignorance; in either of which cases they are and have always been unfit to dictate, to lead opinion, or to receive a following as reliable guides for this world or the next.

If they have been so ignorant or so malicious for nearly nineteen hundred years as to thus systematically misconstrue their own authority—their own "revelation"—to the constant disadvantage of women (and the consequent enfeeblement of the race), surely they can claim no respect for their opinions and no confidence in their divine calling. (See Appendix K.) In trying to shield the Bible the clergy simply convict themselves. (See Appendix L.)

But I incline to the opinion that in the main this view of the case is unfair to the clergy, and that they have followed, in spirit if not literally, the dictates of the Bible as a whole. It is undoubtedly true that the Bible throughout holds woman as an inferior in both mental and moral characteristics; and upon this understanding of it the Fathers built the Church and crystallized the laws.

The Fathers of the Church were as a rule a bad lot themselves. All contemporaneous history and all internal evidence prove this fact: and when we remember that the "Prophets" were almost to a man polygamists; that their belief and practices in this regard were of the order and type of Mormondom to-day, and for the same reasons; that they were slave-holders and slave-stealers; that they believed in a God of infinite cruelty and revenge—of arbitrary will and reasonless barbarity; and that they were licentious and brutal beyond description; (See Appendix M.) it will be easy to understand the position which such men—with these beliefs, practices, mentality, and moral degradation—would accord to women. Every Bible of every people, every history of every race showing like civilization, will show you like results.

In the New Testament we find an effort to readjust old clothes to a new body, some of whose members had grown better and some worse in dogma and belief. Where women are especially dealt with we find them commanded to "be under obedience," and always to subject their wills to the ways and wills of men; while the general tone and treatment are always based upon the assumption that she is an inferior, a secondary creation, and a subject class. (See Appendix N.)

That this is the understanding of the Bible always recognized by the Church (and to-day questioned by only a very small minority who are shrewd enough to see the necessity of revamping it to fit the new public morality and civilization), all history attests; but the vehemence with which the doctrine has been asserted the foregoing pages can only faintly indicate. (See Appendix O.)

But certainly, if for thousands of years the clergy have, as a body, misconstrued or misunderstood the spirit of their own book (to which they have always claimed to possess the only key), they should not blame those who to-day take issue with them upon their information, their dictates, their bases of morality, or their interpretations of the rights of humanity.

If, as they claim to-day, the Bible is the friend of women and no respecter of persons, a conclusion which it took them hundreds of years to reach, it has taken them too long to discover the fact for their guidance to be either a desirable or a safe one for humanity; and the millions of women they have degraded and oppressed in the past are certainly not an argument in favor of their infallibility now. (See Appendix P.)

Let them give way to men who, claiming no right to divine authority or superhuman wisdom, speak in the interest of all humanity the best they know (always acknowledged to be subject to revision for the better); who are not bound back and retarded by the outgrown toggery of the Jewish civilization of David and his time or the Christian dictatorship of Paul. (See Appendix Q.) Acknowledging themselves as false and oppressive interpreters of divine law for centuries past is but a poor recommendation of their ability or integrity for the future.

Whichever horn of the dilemma they accept, there is but one horrible course for the clergy to pursue, and that is to resign in favor of those who have all along been on the right track, without a pretence of divine guidance; who in despite of faith and fagot have made progress possible.

After my lecture on Men, Women, and Gods, in Chicago, I was asked how it would be possible to train children to be good without a belief in the divinity of the Bible; how they could be made to know it is wrong to lie and steal and kill.

The belief that the Bible is the originator of these and like moral ideas, or that Christ was their first teacher, is far from the truth; and it is only another evidence of the duplicity or ignorance of the Church that such a belief obtains or that such a falsehood is systematically taught.

It is too easily forgotten that morals are universal, that Christianity is local. Practical moral ideas grow up very early, and develop with the development of a race. They are the response to the needs of a people, and when formulated have in several cases taken the shape of "commandments" from some unseen power. These necessary practical laws are by degrees attached to those of imaginary value, and all alike are held in esteem as of equal moral worth. By this means a fictitious standard of right and wrong becomes established, and a weakening of confidence in the valueless part results in damage to that portion which was originally the result of wise and necessary legislation. ("Durable morality had been associated with a transitory religious faith. The faith fell into intellectual discredit, and sexual morality shared its decline for a short season. This must always be the natural consequence of building sound ethics on the shifting sands and rotting foundations of theology. It is one of those enormous drawbacks that people seldom take into account when they are enumerating the blessings of superstition."—Morley's "Diderot," p. 71.)

When children (of whatever age) do this or that "because God said so," the precepts taught on this basis, even though they are good, will have no hold upon the man who discovers that their origin was purely human. It is a dangerous experiment and depends wholly upon ignorance for its success. A firm basis of reason in this world is the only solid foundation of moral training.

My Chicago questioner proceeded upon the hypothesis that what of valuable morals are contained in the Bible were a "revelation" to one people, and that their value was dependent upon this origin. For the benefit of those who have been similarly imposed upon, I will cite a few facts in as short space as possible.

Brahmanism, with its two hundred millions of believers, and its Rig-Veda (Bible) composed two thousand four hundred years before Christ, has its rigid code of morals; its theory of creation; its teachings about sin, its revelations, its belief in the ability of the gods to forgive; (Professor Max Muller says that "the consciousness of sin is a leading feature in the religion of the Veda, so is likewise the belief that the gods are able to take away from man the heavy burden of his sins.") its belief that its bible came from God; and its devotees who believe that an infinite God is pleased with the toys of worship, praise, and adulation of man. It has its prayers and hymns, its offerings and sacrifices. Corresponding with our "Trinity" idea the Brahmin has his three great gods; and in place of our "angels" he has his infinite number of little ones. (See Edward Clodd, F.R.A.S., "Childhood of Religions.")

Next, Zoroastrianism, certainly twelve hundred years older than Christ, its legends (quite as authentic as our own) of miracles performed by its founder and his followers; its Zend-Avesta (Bible); its "Supreme Spirit"; its belief in gods and demons who interfere with affairs in this world and who are ever at war with each other; its sacred fires; its Lord; its praise; and its pretence to direct communication in the past with spirits and with gods who gave their Prophet "Commandments." ("In the Gathas or oldest part of the Zend-Avesta, which contains the leading doctrines of Zoroaster, he asks Ormuzd (God) for truth and guidance, and desires to know what he shall do. He is told to be pure in thought, word and deed; to be temperate, chaste, and truthful; to offer prayer to Ormuzd and the powers that fight with him; to destroy all hurtful things; and to do all that will increase the well-being of mankind. Men were not to cringe before the powers of darkness as slaves crouch before a tyrant, they were to meet them upstanding, and confound them by unending opposition and the power of a holy life. 'Oh men if you cling to these commandments which Mazda has given, which are a torment to the wicked and a blessing to the righteous, then there will be victory through them.'"—Max Muller.) It lacks none of the paraphernalia of a "divine institution" ready for business, and we are unable to discount it in either loaves or fishes. It also has its heaven and hell; ("In this old faith there was a belief in two abodes for the departed: heaven, the 'house of the angels' hymns,' and hell, where the wicked were sent. Between the two there was a bridge."—Ibid.) its Messiah or Prophet; its arch fiend or devil; its rites and ceremonies.

Professor Max Muller remarks: "There were periods in the history of the world when the worship of Ormuzd threatened to rise triumphant on the ruins of the temples of all other gods. If the battles of Marathon and Salamis had been lost and Greece had succumbed to Persia, the state religion of the empire of Cyrus, which was the worship of Ormuzd, might have become the religion of the whole civilized world."

In which case my Chicago friend would have asked, "If you destroy a belief in Ormuzd, and that he gave the only supernatural moral law to Zoroaster, how will children ever be taught what is right and what is wrong, and how can they ever know that it is not right to lie and kill and steal?"

"Their creed is of the simplest kind; it is to fear God, to live a life of pure thoughts, pure words, pure deeds, and to die in the hope of a world

to come. It is the creed of those who have lived nearest to God and served him faithfullest in every age, and wherever they dwell who accept it and practice it, they bear witness to that which makes them children of God and brethren of the prophets, among whom Zoroaster was not the least. The Jews were carried away as captives to Babylon some 600 years before Christ, and during the seventy years of their exile there, they came into contact with the Persian religion and derived from it ideas about the immortality of the soul, which their own religion did not contain. They also borrowed from it their belief in a multitude of angels, and in Satan as the ruler over evil spirals." (So you see that even our devil is a borrowed one, and it now seems to be about time to return him with thanks.) "The case with which man believes in unearthly powers working for his hurt prepares a people to admit into its creed the doctrine of evil spirits, and although it is certain that the Jews had no belief in such spirits before their captivity in Babylon, they spoke of Satan (which means an adversary) as a messenger sent from God to watch the deeds of man and accuse them to Him for their wrong-doing. Satan thus becoming by degrees an object of dread, upon whom all the evil which befell man was charged, the maids of the Jews were ripe for accepting the Persian doctrine of Ahriman with his legions of devils. Ahriman became the Jewish Satan, a belief in whom formed part of early Christian doctrine, and is now but slowly dying out. What fearful ills it has caused, history has many a page to tell. The doctrine that Satan, once an angel of light, had been cast from heaven for rebellion against God, and had ever since played havoc among mankind, gave rise to the belief that he and his demons could possess the souls of men and animals at pleasure. Hence grew the belief in wizards and witches, under which millions of creatures, both young and old, were cruelly tortured and put to death. We turn over the smeared pages of this history in haste, thankful that from such a nightmare the world has wakened." (Clodd, F.R.A.S.)

The world has awakened, but the Church still snores on, confident and happy in the belief that she has a devil all her own, and that he is attending strictly to business.

Next we have Buddhism, which numbers more followers than

any other faith. It is five hundred years older than Christianity. It has its prophet or Messiah who was exposed to a tempter, ("Afterward the tempter sent his three daughters, one a winning girl, one a blooming virgin, and one a middle-aged beauty, to allure him, but they could not. Buddha was proof against all the demon's arts, and his only trouble was whether it were well or not to preach his doctrines to men. Feeling how hard to gain was that which he had gained, and how enslaved men were by their passions so that they might neither listen to him nor understand him, he had well-nigh resolved to be silent, but, at the last, deep compassion for all beings made him resolve to tell his secret to mankind, that they too might be free, and he thus became the founder of the most popular religion of ancient or modern times. The spot where Buddha obtained his knowledge became one of the most sacred places in India."—Clodd.) and overcame all evil; its fastings and prayers; its miracles and its visions. Of Buddha's teachings Prof. Max Muller tells us that he used to say, "Nothing on earth is stable, nothing is real. Life is as transitory as a spark of fire, or the sound of a lyre. There must be some supreme intelligence where we could find rest. If I attained it I could bring light to men. If I were free myself I could deliver the world."

Buddha, like Christ, wrote nothing, and the doctrines of the new religion were fixed and written by his disciples after his death. Councils were held afterwards to correct errors and send out missionaries. You will see, therefore, that even "revisions" are not a product of Christianity, and that "revelations" have always been subject to reform to fit the times. ("Two other councils were afterward held for the correction of errors that had crept into the faith, and for sending missionaries into other lands. The last of these councils is said to have been held 251 years before Christ, so that long before Christianity was founded we have this great religion with its sacred traditions of Buddha's words, its councils and its missions, besides, as we shall presently see, many things strangely like the rites of the Roman Catholic Church."—Clodd.)

I will here give a few of the wise or kind or moral commands of

Buddha. If the first were followed in Christian countries we should be a more moral and a less superstitious people than we are to-day.

"*Buddha said: 'The succoring of mother and father, the cherishing of child and wife, and the following of a lawful calling, this is the greatest blessing.'*

" *'The giving alms, a religious life, aid rendered to relations, blameless acts, this, is the greatest blessing.'*

" *'The abstaining from sins and the avoiding them, the eschewing of intoxicating drink, diligence in good deeds, reverence and humility, contentment and gratefulness, this is the greatest blessing.'*

" *'Those who having done these things, become invincible on all sides, attain happiness on all sides. This is the greatest blessing.'*

" *'He who lives a hundred years, vicious and unrestrained, a life of one day is better if a man is virtuous and reflecting.'*

" *'Let no man think lightly of evil, saying in his heart, it will not come near unto me. Even by the falling of water drops a water-pot is filled; the fool becomes full of evil if he gathers it little by little.'*

" *'Not to commit any sin, to do good, and to purify one's mind, that is the teaching of the Awakened.' (This is one of the most solemn verses among the Buddhists.)*

" *'Let us live happily then, not hating those who hate us. Let us dwell free from hatred among men who hate!'*

"*After these doctrines there follow ten commandments, of which the first five apply to all people, and the rest chiefly to such as set themselves apart for a religious life. They are: not to kill; not to steal; not to commit adultery; not to lie; not to get drunk; to abstain from late meals; from public amusements; from expensive dress; from large beds; and to accept neither gold nor silver." (Clodd.)*

Keep in mind that Buddhism lived more than 500 years before Christ.

"*The success of Buddhism was in this: It was a protest against the powers of the priests; it to a large degree broke down caste by declaring that all men are equal, and by allowing any one desiring to live a holy life to become a priest. It abolished sacrifices; made it the duty of all men to honor their parents and care for their children, to be kind to the sick and poor and sorrowing, and to forgive their enemies and return good for evil; it spread a spirit of charity abroad which encompassed the lowest life as well as the highest." (Ibid.)*

With these before him will a Christian suppose that morals are dependent upon our Bible?

Of Confucianism, believed by millions to be essential to their salvation, and one of the three state religions of China, Clodd says: "On the soil of this great country there is crowded nearly half the human race, the most orderly people on the globe. This man (Confucius), who was reviled in life, but whose influence sways the hundreds of millions of China, was born 551 years before Christ. His nature was so beautifully simple and sincere that he would not pretend to knowledge of that which he felt was beyond human reach and thought."

What an earthquake there would be if our clergymen where only to become inoculated with that sort of simple sincerity! His disciples and followers did that for him as has been done in most other cases.

"The sacred books of China are called the Kings, and are five in number, containing treatises on morals, books of rites, poems, and history. They are of great age, perhaps as old as the earliest hymns of the Rig-Veda, and are free from any impure thoughts. (Which is much more than can be said of our own sacred books, which are not so old.) In the Book of Poetry are three hundred pieces, but the design of them all may be embraced in that one sentence, 'Have no depraved thoughts.'

"At the time when Confucius lived, China was divided into a number of petty kingdoms whose rulers were ever quarrelling, and although he became engaged in various public situations of trust, the disorder of the State at last caused him to resign them, and he retired to another part of the country. He then continued the life of a public teacher, instructing men in the simple moral truths by which he sought to govern his own life. The purity of that life, and the example of veneration for the old laws which he set, gathered round him many grave and thoughtful men, who worked with him for the common good."

Confucius said among other wise and moral things: "Coarse rice for food, water to drink, the bended arm for a pillow—happiness may be enjoyed even with these; but without virtue, both riches and honor seem to me like the passing cloud . . . . Our passions shut up the door of our souls against God."

What we are pleased to call "the golden rule," and to look upon as purely Christian, he gave in these words 500 years before Christ was born: "Tsze-kung said, 'What I do not wish men to do to me, I also wish not to do to men.' The Master said, 'You have not attained to that.'

"Such is the power of words, that those uttered by this intensely earnest man, whose work was ended only by death, have kept alive throughout the vast empire of China a reverence for the past and a sense of duty to the present which have made the Chinese the most orderly and moral people in the world."

So much for the great religions that are older than our own and could not have borrowed from us. So much for the moral sentiments of the peoples who developed them, and who live and die happy with them today. It leaves only a small part of this globe and a comparatively small number of its inhabitants who believe in and are guided by the Bible, or by the morality which has grown side-by-side with it.

But there is one other great religion which is of interest to us: (See Appendix R.)

"And the value of Islam, the youngest of the great religions, is that we are able to see how its first simple form became overlaid with legend and foolish superstition, and thus learn how, in like manner, myth and fable have grown around more ancient religions (and around our own).

"For example although Mohammed came into the world like other children, wonderful things are said to have taken place at his birth.

"He never claimed to be a perfect man; he did not pretend to foretell events or to work miracles.

"In spite of all this, his followers said of him, while he was yet living, that he worked wonders, and they believed the golden vision, hinted at in Koran, to have been a real event, although Mohammed said over and over again that it was but a dream.

"This religion is the guide in life and the support in death of one hundred and fifty millions of our fellow creatures; like Christianity, it has its missionaries scattered over the globe, and offers itself as a faith needed by all men.

"The success of Islam was great. Not one hundred years after the death of the prophet, it had converted half the then known world, and its green flag waved from China to Spain. Christianity gave way before it, and has never regained some of the ground then lost, while at this day we see Islam making marked progress in Africa and elsewhere. Travelers tell us that the gain is great when a tribe casts away its idols and embraces Islam. Filth and drunkenness flee away, and the state of the people is bettered in a high degree."

"Muslims have not treated Christ as we have treated Mohammed, for the devout among them never utter his name without adding the touching words, 'on whom be peace.'"

"Mohammed counseled men to live a good life, and to strive after the mercy of God by fasting, charity, and prayer, which he called 'the key of paradise.'"

He abolished the frightful practice of killing female children, and made the family tie more respected.

He said: "A man's true wealth hereafter is the good he has done in this world to his fellow-men. When he dies, people will ask, What property has he left behind him? But the angels will ask, What good deeds has he sent before him?" (Which is a doctrine wholesome and just, so for as it applies to this world, and inculcates the right sort of morals.)

"Mohammed commanded his followers to make no image of any living thing, to show mercy to the weak and orphaned, and kindness to brutes; to abstain from gambling, and the use of strong drink.

"The great truth which he strove to make real to them was that God is one, that, as the Koran says, 'they surely are infidels who say that God is the third of three, for there is no God but one God.'"

He was the great original Unitarian.

"I should add that the wars of Islam did not leave waste and ruin in their path, but that the Arabs, when they came to Europe, alone held aloft the light of learning, and in the once famous schools of Spain, taught 'philosophy, medicine, astronomy, and the golden art of song.'"

We cannot speak so well of the "holy wars" of Christianity.

In speaking of the men who wrote our Bible, Clodd says:

"Nor is it easy to find in what they have said truths which in one form or another, have not been stated by the writers of some of the sacred books into which we have dipped."

I have quoted more fully than had been my intention simply to show the egotistic ignorance of the Christian's claim to possess a religion or a Bible which differs, in any material regard, from several others which are older, and to indicate that moral ideas, precepts, and practices are the property of no special people but are the inevitable result of continued life itself, and the evolution of civilizations however different in outward form and expression. They are the necessary results of human companionship and necessities, and not the fruits of any religion or the "revelation" from on high to any people. As William Kingdom Clifford, F.R.S., in his work on the "Scientific Basis of Morales," very justly says:

"There is more than one moral sense, and what I feel to be right another man may feel to be wrong."

In just the same way our question about the best conscience will resolve itself into a question about the purpose or function of the conscience—why we have got it, and what it is good for.

Now to my mind the simplest and clearest and most profound philosophy that was ever written upon this subject is to be found in the 2d and 3d chapters of Mr. Darwin's 'Descent of Man.' In these chapters it appears that just as most physical characteristics of organisms have been evolved and preserved because they were useful to the individual in the struggle for existence against other individuals and other species, so this particular feeling has been evolved and preserved because it is useful to the tribe or Community in the struggle for existence against other tribes, and against the environment as a whole. The function of conscience is the preservation of the tribe as a tribe. And we shall rightly train our consciences if we learn to approve these actions which tend to the advantage of the community.

The virtue of purity, for example, attains in this way a fairly exact definition: purity in a man is that course of conduct which makes him to be a good husband and father, in a woman that which makes her to be a good wife and mother, or which helps other people so to prepare and keep themselves. It is easy to see how many false ideas and pernicious precepts are swept away by even so simple a definition as that.

In urging the necessity of a more substantial basis of morals than one built upon a theory of arbitrary dictation, he says: "The worship of a deity who is represented as unfair or unfriendly to any portion of the community is a wrong thing, however great may be the threats and promises by which it is commended. And still worse, the reference of right and wrong to his arbitrary will as a standard, the diversion of the allegiance of the moral sense from the community to him, is the most insidious and fatal of social diseases . . . . If I let myself believe anything on insufficient evidence, there may be no great harm done by the mere belief; it may be true after all, or I may never have occasion to exhibit it in outward acts. But I cannot help doing this great wrong toward man, that I make myself credulous. The danger to society is not merely that it should believe wrong things, though that is great enough; but that it should become credulous, and lose the habit of testing things and inquiring into them; for then it must sink back into savagery.

"The harm which is done by credulity in a man is not confined to the fostering of a credulous character in others, and consequent support of false beliefs. Habitual want of care about what I believe leads to habitual want of care in others about the truth of

what is told to me. Men speak the truth to one another when each
reveres the truth in his own mind and in the other's mind; but
how shall my friend revere the truth in my mind when I myself
am careless about it, when I believe things because I want to believe them, and because they are comforting and pleasant? Will he
not learn to cry, 'Peace,' to me, when there is no peace? By such a
course I shall surround myself with a thick atmosphere of falsehood and fraud, and in that I must live. It may matter little to the
me, in my cloud-castle of sweet illusions and daring lies; but it
matters much to Man that I have made my neighbors ready to
deceive. The credulous man is father to the liar . . . .

"We all suffer severely enough from the maintenance and support of false beliefs and the fatally wrong actions which they lead
to; and the evil born when one such belief is entertained is great
and wide. But a greater and wider evil arises when the credulous
character is maintained and supported, when a habit of believing
for unworthy reasons is fostered and made permanent . . . .

"The fact that believers have found joy and peace in believing
gives us the right to say that the doctrine is a comfortable doctrine, and pleasant to the soul; but it does not give us the right to
say that it is true . . . .

"And the question which our conscience is always asking about
that which we are tempted to believe is not, 'is it comfortable and
pleasant?' but, 'Is it true?'"

The sooner moral actions and the necessity of clean, helpful,
and charitable living are put upon a basis more solid and permanent
than theology the better will it be for civilization; and if this chapter
shall, by its light style, attract the attention of those who are too
busy, or are disinclined for any reason whatsoever, to collect from
more profound works the facts here given, I shall be satisfied with
the result, because I shall have done something toward the triumph
of fact over fiction.

We cannot repeat too often nor emphasize too strongly this
one simple fact, that we need all our energy and time to make this
world fit to live in; to make homes where mothers are happy and

children are glad—homes where fathers hasten when their work is done, and are welcomed with a shout of joy.

> *The toilers who wend up the hillside,*
> *The toilers below in the mill*
> *Alike are the victims of priestcraft,*
> *They "do but the Master's will."*
>
> *The Master's will! ah the cunning,*
> *The bitterly cruel device,*
> *To wring from the lowly and burdened*
> *Submission at any price!*
>
> *Submission to tyrants in Russia —*
> *Submission to tyrants in Rome;*
> *The throne and the altar have ever*
> *Combined to despoil the home.*
>
> *But the home is the heaven to live for,*
> *And Love is the God sublime who paints in tints of glory,*
> *Upon the wings of Time*
>
> *This legend, grand and simple,*
> *And true as eternal Right —*
> *No Justice e'er came, from Jury,*
> *Whose verdict was based on might!*
>
> *As high above earth as is heaven;*
> *As high as the stars above*
> *The Church, the chapel, the altar;*
> *Is the home whose God is Love.*

ADDRESS TO THE CLERGY AND OTHERS

Up to the present time I have tried to reply personally to each one who has favored me with a letter of thanks, criticism, or praise of the little book, "Men, Women, and Gods, and Other Lectures," just published, but I find that if I continue to do this I shall have but little time for anything else.

The very unexpected welcome which the book has received prompts me to take this plan and means of replying to many who have honored me by writing me personal letters. First, permit me to thank those, who have written letters of praise and gratitude, and to say that, although I may be unable to reply in a private letter, I am not indifferent to these evidences of your interest, and am greatly helped in my work by your sympathy and encouragement. I have also received most courteous letters from various clergymen who, disagreeing with me, desire to convert me either by mail or personal (private) interviews.

It is wholly impossible for me to grant these requests, since my time and strength are demanded in other work, but I wish to say here what I have written to several of my clerical correspondents, and desire to say to them all.

Although I cannot enter into private correspondence with, nor grant personal interviews to, such a number of our body, I am entirely willing to respond in a public way to any replies to my arguments which come under the following conditions:

1. On page fourteen of the introduction to my book Col. Ingersoll says: "No human being can answer her arguments. There is no answer. All the priests in the world cannot explain away her

objections. There is no explanation. They should remain dumb unless they can show that the impossible is the probable, that slavery is better than freedom, that polygamy is the friend of woman, that the innocent can justly suffer for the guilty, that to persecute for opinion's sake is an act of love and worship."

Now, whenever any one of these gentlemen who wish to convert me will show that the Colonel is wrong in this brief paragraph; whenever they will, in print or in public, refute the arguments to which he refers, and to which they object, I shall not be slow to respond.

2. It must be argument, not personal abuse, and it must be conducted in a courteous manner and tone.

3. It must proceed upon the basis that I am as honest, as earnest, and as virtuous in my motives and intentions as they are in theirs.

Now, surely these gentlemen cannot object to these simple requirements; and since some of them are men whose names are proceeded by a title and followed by several capital letters from D.D. to O.S.F.—(which last I, in my ignorance, guess at as meaning Order of St. Francis, but shall like to be corrected if I am wrong) they must believe that to answer the arguments themselves is both simple and easy.

If they do not so believe they surely have no right to occupy the positions which they do occupy. If they do so believe it will do much more good to answer them publicly, since they have been made publicly, and are already in the hands of several thousand people, who could not be reached by any amount of eloquence poured out on my devoted head in the privacy of my own parlor (or writing-desk).

Therefore, gentlemen, permit me to say to you all that which I have already written to several of you personally—that Col. Ingersoll's paragraph, quoted above, expresses my own views and those of a great many other people, and will continue so to do so long as your efforts to show that he is wrong are only whispered to me behind a fan, or in the strict seclusion of a letter marked "private and personal."

The arguments I have given against the prevailing Christian dogmas and usages, which you uphold, are neither private nor personal, nor shall I allow them to take that phase. Life is too short for me to spend hours day after day in sustaining, in private, a public argument which has never been (and, in my opinion, never will be) refuted. And it would do no good to the thousands whom you are pleased to say you fear will be led astray by my position. You have a magnificent opportunity to lead them back again by honest public letters, or lectures, or sermons, not by an afternoon's chat with me.

And, while I recognize the courtesy of your pressing requests (made, without exception, in the most gentlemanly terms) to permit you to meet me personally and refute my arguments, I feel compelled to say that, unless you are willing to show the courage of your convictions, and the quality of your defense, to the public, I fear they would have no weight with me, and I should have wasted your precious time as well as my own, which I should feel I had no right to do, nor to allow you to do, without this frank statement of the case.

Now, do not suppose that I have the slightest objection to meeting the clergy personally and socially. Upon the contrary, many of my friends are clergymen—even bishops—but candor compels me, to state that up to the present time not one of them has (either privately or otherwise) been able to answer either of the first two lectures in that little book, and as to the third one, no one of them, in my opinion, will ever try to answer it.

Time will show whether I am right in this. In the mean time accept my thanks for your interest, and believe me.
Sincerely, HELEN H. GARDENER.

LETTER TO THE CLEVELAND CONGRESS OF FREETHINKERS, OCTOBER 1885

I send my greetings to the Congress of Freethinkers assembled at Cleveland, and regret, more than I can express that I am unable to be there and hear all the good things you will hear, and see all the earnest workers you will see.

The Freethinkers of America ought to be a very proud and enthusiastic body, when they have in their presidential chair the ablest orator of modern times, and the broadest, bravest, and most comprehensive intellect that has ever been called "Mr. President" in this land of bravery and presidents. Washington was a patriot of whom we are all justly proud. He was liberal in his religion and progressive in his views of personal rights. And yet he had his limitations. To him liberty and personal rights were modified by the words, "free white, adult, males." He got no farther. He who fought for freedom upheld slavery! And yet we are all proud and glad to pay honor and respect to the memory of Washington.

Abraham Lincoln we place still higher on the roll of honor; for, added to his still more liberal religious views, in his conceptions of freedom and justice he had at least two fewer limitations than had the patriot of 1776. He, struck both "free" and "white" from his mental black list, and gave once more an impulse to the human race.

But what shall we say of our president—Ingersoll? A man who

in ten short years has carried mental liberty into every household in America—who is without limitations in religion, and modifies justice with no prefix. A man who, with unequaled oratory, champions Freedom—not the "free white, adult, male freedom of Washington. A man who has breasted a whirlwind of destruction and abuse for Justice—not the 'male, adult' justice of Lincoln, but the freedom and justice, without limitation, for man, woman, and child."

With such a leader, what should not be achieved? With such a champion, what cause could fail? If the people ever place such a man in the White House, the nations of this earth will know, for the first time, the real meaning of a free government under secular administration.

"A government of the people, for the people, by the people," will be more than simply a high-sounding phrase, which, read by the light of the past, was only a bitter mockery to a race in chains; and, read by the light of the present, is a choice bit of grim humor to half of a nation in petticoats. But so long as the taste of the voter is such that he prefers to place in the executive chair a type of man so eminently fitted for private life that when you want to find him you have to shake the chair to see if he is in it, just so long will there be no danger that the lightning will strike so as to deprive the Freethinkers of one man in America who could fill the national executive chair full, and strain the back and sides a little getting in.

Once more I send greetings to the Convention, with the hope that you may have as grand a time as you ought to have, and that Freethought will receive a new impulse from the harmony and enthusiasm of this meeting.

Sincerely, HELEN H. GARDENER.

APPENDICES

Appendix A 1. "For a species increases or decreases in numbers, widens or contracts its habitat, migrates or remains stationary, continues an old mode of life or falls into a new one, under the combined influence of its intrinsic nature and the environing actions, inorganic and organic.

"Beginning with the extrinsic factors, we see that from the outset several kinds of them are variously operative. They need but barely enumerating. We have climate, hot, cold, or temperate, moist or dry, constant or variable. We have surface, much or little of which is available, and the available part of which is fertile in greater or less degree; and we have configuration of surface, as uniform or multiform . . . . On these sets of conditions, inorganic and organic, characterizing the environment, primarily depends the possibility of social evolution."—Spencer, "Principles of Sociology," Vol. 1, p. 10.

2. "These considerations clearly prove that of the two Primary causes of civilization, the fertility of the soil is the one which in the ancient world exercised most influence. But in European civilization, the other great cause, that is to say, climate, has been the most powerful.

"Owing to circumstances which I shall presently state, the only progress which is really effective depends, not upon the bounty of nature, but upon the energy of man. Therefore it is, that the civilization of Europe, which in its earliest stage, was governed by climate, has shown a capacity of development unknown to those civilizations which were originated by soil."—Buckle.

"History of Civilization," vol. 1, p. 36-37. (I wish to state here that I had never read the above from Buckle, nor had I seen anywhere a statement so like my own, at the time mine was written. I read this for the first time while reading the proofs of this chapter, So much for what may appear plagiarism.—H.H.G.)

Appendix B 1. "Napoleon himself was indifferent to Christianity, but he saw that the clergy were friends of despotism."—Buckle.

2. "Thus it is that a careful survey of history will prove that the Reformation made the first progress not in those countries where the people were most enlightened, but in those countries where, from political causes, the clergy were least able to withstand the people."—Buckle.

3. "Christian civilization in the twentieth century of its existence, degrades its women to labor fit only for beasts of the field; harnessing them with dogs to do the most menial labors; it drags them below even this, holding their womanhood up to sale, putting both Church and State sanction upon their moral death; which, in some places, as in the city of Berlin, so far recognizes the sale of woman's bodies for the vilest purposes as part of the Christian religion, that license for this life is refused until they have partaken of the Sacrament; and demands of the '10,000 licensed women of the town' of the city of Hamburg, certificates showing that they regularly attend church and also partake of the sacrament."—Gage.

Even a lower depth than this is reached in England, France, Italy, Switzerland, and Germany, and nearly every country of Europe, says the same writer, "a system of morality which declares 'the necessity' of woman's degradation, and annually sends tens of thousands down to a death from which society grants no resurrection."—Gage.

Appendix C 1. "Sappho flourished B.C. 600, and a little later; and so highly did Plato value, her intellectual, as well as her imaginative endowments, that he assigned her the honors of sage as well as poet; and familiarly entitled her the 'tenth muse.'"—Buckle.

2. "Wilkinson says among no ancient people had women such influence and liberty as among the ancient Egyptians."—Buckle.

3. "The Americans have in the treatment of women fallen below, not only their own democratic principles, but the practice of some parts of the Old World."—Harriet Martineau.

4. "Mr. F. Newman denies that Christianity has improved the position of women; and he observes that, 'with Paul, the sole reason for marriage is, that a man may, without sin, vent his sensual desires. He teaches that, but for this object, it would be better not to marry;' and he takes no notice of the social pleasures of marriage. Newman says: 'In short, only in countries where Germanic sentiment has taken root do we see marks of any elevation of the female sex superior to that of Pagan antiquity.'"—Buckle.

5. "Female voices are never heard in the Russian churches; their place is supplied by boys; women do not yet stand high enough in the estimation of the churches . . . . to be permitted to sing the praises of God in the presence of men."—Kohl.

6. "Christianity diminished the influence of women."—Neander, "Hist. of the Church."

Appendix D Within the reign of the present sovereign Mrs. Gage tells us of a young girl being ordered by the Petty Sessions Bench back to the "service" of a landlord, from whom she had run away because such service meant the sacrifice of her honor. She refused to go and was put in jail.

Appendix E 1. "Women were taught by the Church and State alike, that the Feudal Lord or Seigneur had a right to them, not only against themselves, but as against any claim of husband or father. The law known as Marchetta, or Marquette, compelled newly-married women to a most dishonorable servitude. They were regarded as the rightful prey of the Feudal Lord from one to three days after their marriage, and from this custom, the oldest son of the serf was held as the son of the lord, 'as perchance it was he who begat him' From this nefarious degradation of woman, the custom of Borough-English arose, in which the youngest son became the heir . . . . France, Germany, Prussia, England, Scotland, and all Christian countries where feudalism existed, held to the enforcement of Marquette. The lord deemed this right as fully his as he did the claim to half the crops of the land, or to half the wool of the sheep. More than one reign of terror arose in France from the enforcement of this law, and the uprisings of the peasantry over Europe during the twelfth century, and the fierce Jacquerie, or Peasant Wars, of the fourteenth century in France owed their origin, among other causes, to the enforcement of these claims by the lords upon the newly-married wife. The edicts of Marly transplanted that claim to America when Canada was under the control of France. To persons not conversant with the history of feudalism, and of the Church for the first fifteen hundred years of its existence, it will seem impossible that such foulness could ever have been part of Christian civilization. That the crimes they have been trained to consider the worst forms of heathendom could have existed in Christian Europe, upheld by both Church and State for more than a thousand five hundred years, will strike most people with incredulity. Such, however, is the truth; we can but admit well-attested facts of history, how severe a blow they strike our preconceived beliefs.

"Marquette was claimed by the Lords Spiritual, ("In days to come people will be slow to believe that the law among Christian nations went beyond anything decreed concerning the olden slavery; that it wrote down as an actual right the most grievous outrage that could ever wound man's heart. The Lords Spiritual (clergy) had this right no less than the Lords Temporal. The parson, being a lord, expressly claimed the first fruits of the bride, but was willing to sell his right to the husband. The Courts of Berne openly maintain that this right grew up naturally."—Michelet, "La Sorcerie," p. 62.) as well as by the Lords Temporal. The Church, indeed, was the bulwark of this base feudal claim. With the power of penance and excommunication in its grasp, this demand could neither have originated nor been sustained unless sanctioned by the Church . . . . These customs of feudalism were the customs of

Christianity during many centuries. (One of the Earls of Crawford, known as the 'Earl Brant,' in the sixteenth century, was probably among the last who openly claimed by right the literal translation of droit de Jambage.) These infamous outrages upon woman were enforced under Christian law by both Church and State.

"The degradation of the husband at this infringement of the lord spiritual and temporal upon his marital right, has been pictured by many writers, but history has been quite silent upon the despair and shame of the wife. No hope appeared for woman anywhere. The Church . . . . dragged her to the lowest depths, through the vileness of its priestly customs . . . . We who talk of the burning of wives upon the funeral pyres of husbands in India, may well turn our eyes to the records of Christian countries."—Matilda Joslyn Gage in "Woman, Church, and State."

2. From this point Mrs. Gage calls attention to the various efforts to throw off this degrading custom. The women held meetings at night, and among other things travestied the celebration of Mass and other Church customs; but the end and aim of these meetings being a protest and rebellion against Marquette, the clergy called those who took part in them "witches"; ("There are few superstitions which have been so universal as a belief in witchcraft. The severe theology of paganism despised the wretched superstition, which has been greedily believed by millions of Christians."—Buckle.) and then and there began the persecution which the Church carried on against women under this disguise (under Catholic and Protestant rule alike), which extended down to the latter part of the last century, with its list of horrors and indignities extending over all Christian countries and blossoming in all their vigor in our own eastern States, upheld by Luther, John Wesley, and Baxter, who unfortunately had not at that time entered into the everlasting rest of the Saints. And, true to these noble and wise leaders, the Churches which they founded are to-day expressing the same sentiments (in principle) in regard to the honor and dignity and position of woman. The arguments of the Rev.

Dr. Craven, the prosecutor in the famous Presbyterian trial of 1876, which are given by Mrs. Gage, together with numerous other similar ones, fully establish the fact that woman is to the Church what she always was—so far as secular law will permit. And numerous instances (such as the Buckley exhibition at the last Methodist Conference, in which he was sustained by the Conference) prove that they have learned nothing since 1876.

3. I wish I might copy here the sermon to women which the Rev. Knox-Little, the well-known High-Church clergyman of England, preached when in this country in 1880, in which he said, "There is no crime which a man can commit which justifies his wife in leaving him. It is her duty to subject herself to him always, and no crime that he can commit can justify her lack of obedience." Although a little balder in statement than are most utterances of orthodox clergymen in this age, yet in sentiment and in the reason given for it the echo of "Amen" comes from every pulpit where a believer in original sin, vicarious atonement, or the inspiration of the Bible has a representative and a voice. If self-respect or honor is ever to be the lot of woman, it will not be until her foot is on the neck of orthodoxy, and when the Bible ranks where it belongs in the field of literature.

Appendix F 1. "The French government, about the middle of the eighteenth century, seems to have reached the maturity of its wickedness, allowing if not instigating religious persecutions of so infamous a nature that they would not be believed if they were not attested by documents of the courts in which the sentences were passed."—Buckle.

2. Of Louis XV, the eminently Christian king of France, Buckle says: "His harem cost more than 100,000,000 francs, and was composed of little girls. He was constantly drunk," and "turned out his own illegitimate children to prostitute themselves."

3. "It will hardly be believed that, when sulfuric ether was first used to lessen the pains of childbirth, it was objected to as 'a

profane attempt to abrogate the primeval curse pronounced upon woman.' ... The injury which the theological principle has done to the world is immense. It has prevented men from studying the laws of nature."—Buckle.

Appendix G 1.The narrow range of their sympathies (the clergy's), and the intellectual servitude they have accepted, render them peculiarly unfitted for the office of educating the young, which they so persistently claim, and which, to the great misfortune of the world, they were long permitted to monopolize . . . . The almost complete omission from female education of those studies which most discipline and strengthen the intellect, increases the difference, while at the same time it has been usually made a main object to imbue them with a passionate faith in traditional opinions, and to preserve them from all contact with opposing views. But contracted knowledge and imperfect sympathy are not the sole fruits of this education. It has always been the peculiarity of a certain kind of theological teaching, that it inverts all the normal principles of judgment and absolutely destroys intellectual diffidence. On other subjects we find, if not a respect for honest conviction, at least some sense of the amount of knowledge that is requisite to entitle men to express an opinion on great controversies. A complete ignorance of the subject-matter of a dispute restrains the confidence of dogmatism; and an ignorant person who is aware that, by much reading and thinking in spheres of which he has himself no knowledge, his educated neighbor has modified or rejected opinions which that ignorant person had been taught, will, at least if he is a man of sense or modesty, abstain from compassionating the benighted condition of his more instructed friend. But on theological questions this has never been so.

"Unfaltering belief being taught as the first of duties, and all doubt being usually stigmatized as criminal or damnable, a state of mind is formed to which we find no parallel in other fields. Many men and most women, though completely ignorant of the very rudiments of biblical criticism, historical research, or scientific discoveries, though they have never read a single page, or understood a single proposition of the writings of those whom they condemn, and have absolutely no rational knowledge either of the arguments by which their faith is defended, or of those by which it has been impugned, will nevertheless adjudicate with the utmost confidence upon every polemical question, denounce, hate, pity, or pray for the conversion of all who dissent from what they have been taught, assume, as a matter beyond the faintest possibility of doubt, that the opinions they have received without inquiry must be true, and that the opinions which others have arrived at by inquiry must be false, and make it a main object of their lives to assail what they call heresy in every way in their power, except by examining the grounds on which it rests. It is possible that the great majority of voices that swell the clamor against every book which is regarded as heretical, are the voices of those who would deem it criminal even to open that book, or to enter into any real, searching, and impartial investigation of the subject to which it relates. Innumerable pulpits support this tone of thought, and represent, with a fervid rhetoric well fitted to excite the nerves and imaginations of women, the deplorable condition of all who deviate from a certain type of opinions or emotions; a blind propagandism or a secret wretchedness penetrates into countless households, poisoning the peace of families, chilling the mental confidence of husband and wife, adding immeasurably to the difficulties which every searcher into truth has to encounter, and diffusing far and wide intellectual timidity, disingenuousness, and hypocrisy."—Lecky.

2. "The clergy, with a few honorable exceptions, have in all modern countries been the avowed enemies of the diffusion of knowledge, the danger of which to their own profession they, by a certain instinct, seem always to have perceived."—Buckle.

3. "In the fourth century there arose monarchism, and in the sixth century the Christians succeeded in cutting off the last ray of knowledge, and shutting up the schools of Greece. Then followed a long period of theology, ignorance, and vice."—Buckle.

4. "Contempt for human sciences was one of the first features of Christianity. It had to avenge itself of the outrages of philosophy; it feared that spirit of investigation and doubt, that confidence of man in his own reason, the pest alike of all religious creeds. The light of the natural sciences was ever odious to it, and was ever regarded with a suspicious eye, as being a dangerous enemy to the success of miracles; and there is no religion that does not oblige its sectaries to follow some physical absurdities. The triumph of Christianity was thus the final signal of the entire decline both of the sciences and of philosophy."— "Progress of the Human Mind," Condorcet.

"Accordingly it ought not to astonish us that Christianity, though unable in the sequel to prevent their reappearance in splendor after the invention of printing, was at this period sufficiently powerful to accomplish their ruin."—Ibid.

"In the disastrous epoch at which we are now arrived, we shall see the human mind rapidly descending from the height to which it had raised itself . . . . Everywhere was corruption, cruelty, and perfidy . . . . Theological reveries, superstitions, delusions, are become the sole genius of man, religious intolerance his only morality; and Europe, crushed between sacerdotal tyranny and military despotism, awaits in blood and in tears the moment when the revival of light shall restore it to liberty, to humanity, and to virtue . . . . The priests held human learning in contempt . . . . Fanatic armies laid waste the provinces. Executioners, under the guidance of legates and priests, put to death those whom the soldiers had spared. A tribunal of monks was established, with power of condemning to the stake whoever should be suspected of making use of his reason . . . . All sects, all governments, every species of authority, inimical as they were to each other in every point else, seemed to be of accord in granting no quarter to the exercise of reason . . . . Meanwhile education, being everywhere subjected (to the clergy), had corrupted everywhere the general understanding, by clogging the reason of children with the weight of the religious prejudices of their country . . . . In the eighth century an ignorant pope had persecuted a deacon for contending that the earth was round, in opposition to the opinion of the rhetorical Saint Austin. In the fifteenth, the ignorance of another pope, much more inexcusable, delivered Galileo into the hands of the inquisition, accused of having proved the diurnal and annual motion of the earth. The greatest genius that modern Italy has given to the sciences, overwhelmed with age and infirmities, was obliged to purchase his release from punishment and from prison, by asking pardon of God for having taught men better to understand his works."—Ibid.

Appendix H 1. Fenelon, a celebrated French clergyman and writer of the seventeenth century, discouraged the acquisition of knowledge by women.—See Hallam's. "Lit. of Europe."

2. "Perhaps it is to the spirit of Puritanism that we owe the little influence of women, and the consequent inferiority of their education."—Buckle.

3. "In England (1840) a distrust and contempt for reason prevails amongst religious circles to a wide extent; many Christians think it almost a matter of duty to decry the human faculties as poor, mean, and almost worthless; and thus seek to exalt piety at the expense of intelligence."—Morell's "Hist. of Speculative Phil."

4. "That women are more deductive than men, because they think quicker than men, is a proposition which some people will not relish, and yet it may be proved in a variety of ways. Indeed nothing could prevent its being universally admitted except the fact that the remarkable rapidity with which women think is obscured by that miserable, that contemptible, that preposterous system, called their education, in which valuable things are carefully kept from them, and trifling things carefully taught to them, until their fine and nimble minds are too often irretrievably injured."—Buckle.

Appendix I 1. "The Roman (Pagan) religion was essentially domestic, and it was a main object of the legislator to surround marriage with every circumstance of dignity and solemnity.

Monogamy was from the earliest times, strictly enjoined, and it was one of the great benefits that have resulted from the expansion of Roman power, that it made this type dominant in Europe. In the legends of early Rome we have ample evidence both of the high moral estimate of women, and of their prominence in Roman life. The tragedies of Lucretia and of Virginia display a delicacy of honor, a sense of the supreme excellence of unsullied purity which no Christian nation could surpass."—Lecky, "European Morals," Vol. I, p. 316.

2. "Marriage (under Christian rule) was viewed in its coarsest and most degraded form. The notion of its impurity took many forms, and exercised for some centuries an extremely wide influence over the Church."—Ibid, p. 343.

Appendix J 1. "We are continually told that civilization and Christianity have restored to the woman her just rights. Meanwhile the wife is the actual bond-servant of her husband; no less so, as far as legal obligation goes, than slaves commonly so called. She vows a lifelong obedience to him at the altar, and is held to it all through her life by law. Casuists may say that the obligation of obedience stops short of participation in crime, but it certainly extends to everything else. She can do no act whatever but by his permission, at least tacit. She can acquire no property but for him; the instant it becomes hers even if by inheritance, it becomes ipso facto his. In this respect the wife's position under the common law of England is worse than that of slaves in the laws of many countries; by the Roman law, for example, a slave might have peculium, which, to a certain extent, the law guaranteed him for his exclusive use."—Mill.

2. Speaking of self-worship which leads to brutality toward others, Mill says "Christianity will never practically teach it" (the equality of human beings) "While it sanctions institutions grounded on an arbitrary preference for one human being over another."

"The morality of the first ages rested on the obligation to submit to power; that of the ages next following, on the right of the weak to the forbearance and protection of the strong. How much longer is one form of society and life to content itself with the morality made for another? We have had the morality of submission, and the morality of chivalry and generosity; the time is now come for the morality of justice."—Ibid.

"Institutions, books, education, society all go on training human beings for the old, long after the new has come; much more when it is only coming."—Ibid.

"There have been abundance of people, in all ages of Christianity, who tried ... to convert us into a Sort of Christian Mussulmans, with the Bible for a Koran, prohibiting all improvement; and great has been their power, and many have had to sacrifice their lives in resisting them. But they have been resisted, and the resistance has made us what we are, and will yet make us what we are to be."—Ibid.

Appendix K "In this tendency (to depreciate extremely the character and position of woman) we may detect in part the influence of the earlier Jewish writings, in which it is probable that most impartial observers will detect evident traces of the common oriental depreciation of women. The custom of money-purchase to the father of the bride was admitted. Polygamy was authorized, and practiced by the wisest men on an enormous scale. A woman was regarded as the origin of human ills. A period of purification was appointed after the birth of every child; but, by a very significant provision, it was twice as long in the case of a female as of a male child (Levit. xii. 1-5). The badness of men, a Jewish writer emphatically declared, is better than the goodness of women Ecclesiastics xlii. 14). The types of female excellence exhibited in the early period of Jewish history are in general of a low order, and certainly far inferior to those of Roman history or Greek poetry; and the warmest eulogy of a woman in the Old Testament is probably that which was bestowed upon her who, with circumstances of the most exaggerated treachery, had murdered the sleeping fugitive who had taken refuge under her roof."—Lecky, "European Morals," vol. 1, p. 357.

Appendix L 1. "Mr. F. Newman, who looks on toleration as the result intellectual progress, says Nevertheless, not only does the Old Testament justify bloody persecution, but the New teaches that God will visit men with fiery vengeance for holding an erroneous creed."—Buckle.

2. "The first great consequence of the decline of priestly influence was the rise of toleration . . . . I suspect that the impolicy of persecution was perceived before its wickedness."—Ibid.

3. "While a multitude of scientific discoveries, critical and historical researches, and educational reforms have brought thinking men face to face with religious problems of extreme importance, women have been almost absolutely excluded from their influence."—Lecky.

4. "The domestic unhappiness arising from difference of belief was probably almost or altogether unknown in the world before the introduction of Christianity . . . . The deep and widening chasm between the religious opinions of most highly educated men, and of the immense majority of women is painfully apparent. Whenever any strong religious fervor fell upon a husband or a wife, its first effect was to make a happy union impossible."—Ibid.

5. "The combined influence of the Jewish writings (Old Testament) and of that ascetic feeling which treated woman as the chief source of temptation to man, caused her degradation . . . . In the writings of the Fathers, woman was represented as the door of hell, as the mother of all human ills. She should be ashamed at the very thought that she is a woman. She should live in continual penance, on account of the curse she has brought into the world. She should be ashamed of her dress and especially ashamed of her beauty."—Ibid.

Appendix M 1. "The writers of the Middle Ages are full of accounts of nunneries that were like brothels . . . . The inveterate prevalence of incest among the clergy rendered it necessary again and again to issue the most stringent enactments that priests should not be permitted to live with their mothers or sisters . . . . An Italian bishop of the tenth century epigrammatically described the morals of his time, when he declared, that if he were to enforce the canons against unchaste people administering ecclesiastical rites, no one would be left in the Church except the boys."—Lecky.

2. In the middle of the sixteenth century "the majority of the clergy were nearly illiterate, and many of them addicted to drunkenness and low vices."—Hallam, "Const. Hist. of Eng."

3. "The clergy have ruined Italy."—Brougham, "Pol. Phil."

4. "It was a significant prudence of many of the lay Catholics, who were accustomed to insist that their priests should take a concubine for the protection of the families of the parishioners . . . . It can hardly be questioned that the extreme frequency of illicit connections among the clergy tended during many centuries most actively to lower the moral tone of laity . . . . An impure chastity was fostered, which continually looked upon marriage in its coarsest light . . . . Another injurious consequence resulting, in a great measure, from asceticism, was a tendency to depreciate extremely the character and the position of woman."—Lecky.

Appendix N "The great and main duty which a wife, as a wife, ought to learn, and so learn as to practice it, is to be subject to her own husband . . . . There is not any husband to whom this honor of submission is not due; no personal infirmity, forwardness of nature; no, not even on the point of religion, doth deprive him of it."—Fergusson on "the Epistles."

2. "The sum of a wife's duty unto her husband is subjection."—Abernethy.

3. "We shall be told, perhaps, that religion imposes the duty of obedience (upon wives); as every established fact which is too bad to admit of any other defense, is always presented to us as an injunction of religion. The Church, it is true, enjoins it in her formularies."—Mill.

"The principle of the modern movement in morals and in politics, is that conduct, and conduct alone, entitles to respect: that not what men are, but what they do constitutes their claim to deference; that, above all, merit and not birth is the only rightful claim to power and authority."—Ibid.

"Taking the care of people's lives out of their own hands and relieving them from the consequences of their own acts, saps the very foundation of the self-respect and self-control which are the essential conditions both of individual prosperity and of social virtue."—Ibid.

"Inferior classes of men always, at heart, feel disrespect toward those who are subject to their power."—Ibid.

4. "Among those causes of human improvement that are of most importance to the general welfare, must be included the total annihilation of the prejudices which have established between the sexes an inequality of right, fatal even to the party which it favors. In vain might we seek for motives to justify the principle, in difference of physical organization, of intellect, or of moral sensibility. It had at first no other origin but abuse of strength, and all the attempts which have since been made to support it are idle sophisms"—"Progress of the Human Mind," Condorcet.

5. Notwithstanding the work of such men is the Encyclopedists of France and other liberal thinkers for the proper recognition of women, the Church had held her grip so tight that upon the passage of the bill, as late as 1848, giving to married women the right to own their own property, the most doleful prophesies went up as to the just retribution that would fall upon women for their wicked insubordination, and upon the men who had defied divine commands so far is to pass such a law. A recent writer tells us that Wm. A. Stokes, in talking to a lady whom he blamed for its passage, said: "We hold you responsible for that law, and I tell you now you will live to rue the day when you opened such a Pandora's box in your native State, and cast such an apple of discord into every family of the State."

And the sermons that were preached against it—the prophecies of deacon and preacher—were so numerous, so denunciatory, and so violent that they form a queer and interesting chapter in the history of the attitude of the Church toward women, and illustrate, in our own time, how persistent it has been in its efforts to prevent woman from sharing in the benefits of the higher civilization of the nineteenth century.

But fortunately for women, Infidels are more numerous than they ever were before, and the power of the Church is dying of dry rot, or as Col. Ingersoll wittily says, of the combined influence of softening of the brain and ossification of the heart.

Appendix O "St. Gregory the Great describes the virtue of a priest, who through motives of piety had discarded his wife . . . . Their wives, in immense numbers, were driven forth with hatred and with scorn . . . . Pope Urban II. gave license to the nobles to reduce to slavery the wives of priests who refused to abandon them."—Lecky.

Appendix P 1. "Hallam denies that respect for women is due to Christianity."—Buckle.

2. "In England, wives are still occasionally led to the market by a halter around the neck to be sold by the husband to the highest bidder."—Ibid.

"The sale of a wife with a halter around her neck is still a legal transaction in England. The sale must be made in the cattle market, as if she were a mare, all women being considered as mares by old English law, and indeed called 'mares' in certain counties where genuine old English law is still preserved."—Borrow.

3. "Contempt for woman, the result of clerical teaching, is shown in myriad forms."—Gage.

4. "The legal subordination of one sex to another is wrong in itself, and is now one of the chief hindrances to human improvement."—John Stuart Mill.

5. "I have no relish for a community of goods resting on the doctrine, that what is mine is yours, but what is yours is not mine; and I should prefer to decline entering into such a compact with

anyone, though I were myself the person to profit by it."—
Ibid.

It will take a long time for that sort of morality to filter into
the skull of the Church, and when it does the skull will burst.

6. "Certain beliefs have been inculcated, certain crimes invented,
   in order to intimidate the masses. Hence the Church made
   free thought the worst of sins, and the spirit of inquiry the
   worst of blasphemies . . . . As late as the time of Bunyan the
   chief doctrine inculcated from the pulpit was obedience to the
   temporal power . . . . All these influences fell with crushing
   weight on woman."—Matilda Joslyn Gage in "Hist. Woman
   Suffrage."

7. "Taught that education for her was indelicate and irreligious,
   she has been kept in such gross ignorance as to fall a prey to
   superstition, and to glory in her degradation . . . . Such was
   the prejudice against a liberal education for women, that the
   first public examination of a girl in geometry (1829) created
   as bitter a storm of ridicule as has since assailed women who
   have entered the law, the pulpit, or the medical profession."—
   Ibid.

Appendix Q 1. "The five writers to whose genius we owe the first
   attempt at comprehensive views of history were Bolingbroke,
   Montesquieu, Voltaire, Hume, and Gibbon. Of these the
   second was but a cold believer in Christianity, if, indeed, he
   believed in it at all; and the other four were avowed and
   notorious infidels."—Buckle.

2 "Here, then, we have the starting-point of progress—skepticism
   . . . . All, therefore, that men want is no hindrance from their
   political and religious rulers . . . . Until common minds doubt
   respecting religion they can never receive any new scientific
   conclusion at variance with it—as Joshua and Copernicus."—
   Ibid.

3. "The immortal work of Gibbon, of which the sagacity is, if
   possible, equal to the learning, did find readers, but the illus-
   trious author was so cruelly reviled by men who called them-

selves Christians, that it seemed doubtful if, after such an example, subsequent writers would hazard their comfort and
happiness by attempting to write philosophic history.
Middleton wrote in 1750 . . . . As long as the theological
spirit was alive nothing could be effected."—Ibid.

4. "The questions which presented themselves to the acuter minds
of a hundred years ago were present to the acuter minds who
lived hundreds of years before that . . . . But the Church had
known how to deal with intellectual insurgents, from Abelard
in the twelfth century down to Bruno and Vanini in the seventeenth. They were isolated, and for the most part submis-
sive; and if they were not, the arm of the Church was very long
and her grasp mortal . . . .

"They (the thinkers) could have taught Europe earlier than
the Church allowed it to learn, that the sun does not go round the
earth, and that it is the earth which goes round the sun . . . . After
the middle of the last century the insurrection against the
pretensions of the Church and against the doctrines of Christianity
was marked in one of its most important phases by a new, and
most significant, feature . . . . It was an advance both in knowledge
and in moral motive . . . . The philosophical movement was
represented by "Diderot" (leading the Encyclopedist circle.) ...
Broadly stated the great central moral of it was this: that human
nature is good, that the world is capable of being made a desirable
abiding-place. and that the evil of the world is the fruit of bad
education and bad institutions. This cheerful doctrine now strikes
on the ear as a commonplace and a truism. A hundred years ago in
France it was a wonderful gospel, and the beginning of a new
dispensation . . . . into what fresh and unwelcome sunlight it
brought the articles of the old theology . . . . Every social
improvement since has been the outcome of that new doctrine in
one form or another . . . . The teaching of the Church paints men
as fallen and depraved. The deadly chagrin with which churchmen
saw the new fabric rising was very natural . . . . The new secular
knowledge clashed at a thousand points, alike in letter and spirit,

with the old sacred lore . . . . A hundred years ago this perception was vague and indefinite, but there was an unmistakable apprehension that the Catholic ideal of womanhood was no more adequate to the facts of life, than Catholic views about science, or popery, or labor, or political order and authority."—Morley.

And it took the rising infidels to discover the fact. See Morley, "Diderot," p. 76.

"The greatest fact in the intellectual history of the eighteenth century is the decisive revolution that overtook the sustaining conviction of the Church. The central conception, that the universe was called into existence only to further its Creator's purpose toward man, became incredible (by the light of the new thought). What seems to careless observers a mere metaphysical dispute was in truth. and still is, the decisive quarter of the great battle between theology and a philosophy reconcilable with science."—Morley.

"The man who ventured to use his mind (Diderot) was thrown into the dungeon at Vincennes."—Ibid.

5. "Those thinkers (Voltaire, Rousseau, and Diderot) taught men to reason; reasoning well leads to acting well; justness in the mind becomes justice in the heart. Those toilers for progress labored usefully . . . . The French Revolution was their soul. It was their radiant manifestation. It came from them; we find them everywhere in that blest and superb catastrophe, which formed the conclusion of the past and the opening of the future . . . . The new society, the desire for equality and concession, and that beginning of fraternity which called itself tolerance, reciprocal good-will the just accord of men and rights, reason recognized as the supreme law, the annihilation of prejudices and fixed opinions, the serenity of souls, the spirit of indulgence and of pardon, harmony, peace—behold what has come from them!"—Victor Hugo, "Oration on Voltaire."

Appendix R "He (Mohammed) promulgated a mass of fables, which he pretended to have received from heaven . . . . After enjoying for twenty years a power without bounds, and of which there exists no other example, he announced publicly, that, if he had committed any act of injustice, be was ready to make reparation. All were silent . . . . He died; and the enthusiasm which he communicated to his people will be seen to change the face of three-quarters of the globe . . . . I shall add that the religion of Mohammed is the most simple in its dogmas, the least absurd in its practices, above all others tolerant in its principles."—Condorcet.

Appendix S The claim is so often and so boldly made that Infidelity produces crime, and that Christianity, or belief, or faith, makes people good, that the following statistics usually produce a rather chilly sensation in the believer when presented in the midst of an argument based upon the above mentioned claim. I have used it with effect. The person upon whom it is used will never offer that argument to you again. The following statistics were taken from the British Parliamentary reports, made on the instance of Sir John Trelawney, in 1873:

ENGLAND AND WALES: Criminals in England and Wales in 1873–146,146

SECTARIAN AND INFIDEL POPULATION OF THE SAME: Church of England–6,933,935; Dissenters–7,235.158; Catholics–1,500,000; Jews–57,000; Infidels–7,000,000

RELIGIOUS PERSUASIONS OF CRIMINALS OF THE SAME: Church of England–96,097; Catholics–35,581; Dissenters–10,648; Jews–256; Infidels–296.

CRIMINALS TO 100,000 POPULATION: Catholics–2,500; Church of England–1,400; Dissenters–150; Infidels–5.

These statistics are taken from the report of the British Parliament, which, for learning and intelligence, as a deliberative body, has not its superior, if it has its equal, in the world, and it is surely a sufficiently Christian body to be accepted as authority in this matter, since a large number of its members are clergymen. These statistics hardly sustain the allegation that "Infidelity is coupled with impurity."

We are willing to stand upon our record. But, lest it be claimed that this is a British peculiarity, allow me to defer to the patriotic sentiment of my readers by one other little set of tables which, while not complete, is equally as suggestive.

"In sixty-six different prisons, jails, reformatories, refuges, penitentiaries, and lock-ups there are for the years given in reports, 41,335 men and boys, women and girls, of the following religious sects: *Catholics–16,431; Church of England–9,975; Eighteen other Protestant denominations–14,811; Universalists–5; Jews, Chinese, and Mormons–110; Infidels (two so-called, one avowed)–3.*

"These included the prisons of Iowa, Michigan, Tennessee, New York, Pennsylvania, Connecticut, Indiana, Illinois, and Canada."

Present these two tables to those who assure you that crime follows in the wake of Infidelity, and you will have time to take a comfortable nap before your Christian friend returns to the attack or braces up after the shock sustained by his sentiments and inflicted by these two small but truly suggestive tables.

One cold fact like this will inoculate one of the faithful with more modesty than an hour of usual argument based upon the assumptions of the clergy and the ignorance of his hearers.

Infidels are not perfect. Many of them need reconstruction sadly, but the above data seem to indicate that they compare rather favorably with their fellow-men in the matter of good citizenship.
Appendix T "Moreover, as Goethe has already shown, the celebrated Mosaic moral precepts, the so-called Ten Commandments, were not upon the tables upon which Moses wrote the laws of the covenant which God made with his people.

"Even the extraordinary diversity of the many religions diffused over the surface of the earth suffices to show that they can stand in no necessary connection with morals, as it is well known that wherever tolerably well-ordered political and social conditions exist, the moral precepts in their essential principles are the same, whilst when such conditions are wanting, a wild and irregular confusion, or even an entire deficiency of moral notions is met with. ("In China, where people are, as is well-known, very indifferent or tolerant in religions matters, this fine proverb is current:

Religions are various, but reason is one, and we are all brothers.")
History also shows incontrovertibly that religion and morality have
by no means gone hand in hand in strength and development, but
that even contrariwise the most religious times and countries have
produced the greatest number of crimes and sins against the laws
of morality, and indeed, as daily experience teaches, still produce
them. The history of nearly all religions is filled with such horrible
abominations, massacres, and boundless wickedness of every kind
that at the mere recollection of them the heart of a philanthropist
seems to stand still, and we turn with disgust and horror from a
mental aberration which could produce such deeds. If it is urged
in vindication of religion that it has advanced and elevated human
civilization, even this merit appears very doubtful in presence of
the facts of history, and at least as very rarely or isolatedly the case.
In general, however, it cannot be denied that most systems of religion have proved rather inimical than friendly to civilization. For
religion, as already stated, tolerates no doubt, no discussion, no
contradiction, no investigations, by those eternal pioneers of the
future of science and intellect! Even the simple circumstance that
our present state of culture has already long since left far behind it
all and even the highest intellectual ideals established and elabo-
rated by former religions may show how little intellectual progress
is influenced by religion. Mankind is perpetually being thrown to
and fro between science, and religion, but it advances more intellectually, morally and physically in proportion as it turns away
from religion and to science.

It is therefore clear that for our present age and for the future
a foundation must be sought and found for culture and morality,
different from that which can be furnished to us by religion. It is
not the fear of God that acts amelioratingly or ennoblingly upon
manners, of which the middle ages furnish us with a striking proof;
but the ennobling of the conception of the world in general which
goes hand in hand with the advance of civilization. Let us then
give up making a show of the profession of hypocritical words of
faith, the only purpose of which seems to be that they may be

continually shown to be lies by the actions and deeds of their professors! The man of the future will feel far more happy and contented when he has not to contend at every step of his intellectual forward development with those tormenting contradictions between knowledge and faith which plague his youth, and occupy his mature age unnecessarily with the slow renunciation of the notions which he imbibed in his youth. What we sacrifice to God, we take away from mankind, and absorb a great part of his best intellectual powers in the pursuit of an unattainable goal. At any rate, the least that we can expect in this respect from the state and society of the future is a complete separation between ecclesiastical and worldly affairs, or an absolute emancipation of the state and the school from every ecclesiastical influence. Education must be founded upon knowledge, not upon faith; and religion itself should be taught in the public schools only as religious history and as an objective or scientific exposition of the different religious systems prevailing among mankind. Any one who, after such an education, still experiences the need of a definite law or rule of faith may then attach himself to any religious sect that may seem good to him, but cannot claim that the community should bear the cost of this special fancy!

"As regards Christianity, or the Paulinism which is falsely called Christianity, it stands, by its dogmatic portion or contents, in such striking and irreconcilable, nay absolutely absurd contradiction with all the acquisitions and principles of modern science that its future tragical fate can only be a question of time. But even its ethical contents or its moral principles are in no way essentially distinguished above those of other peoples, and were equally well and in part better known to mankind even before its appearance. Not only in this respect, but also in its supposed character as the world-religion, it is excelled by the much older and probably most widely diffused religious system in the world, the celebrated Buddhism, which recognizes neither the idea of a personal God, nor that of a personal duration, and nevertheless teaches an extremely pure, amiable, and even ascetic morality. The doctrine of Zoroaster or Zarathustra also, 1800 years B.C., taught the principles of humanity and toleration for those of different modes of thinking in a manner and purity which were unknown to the Semitic religions and especially to Christianity. Christianity originated and spread, as is well-known, at a time of general decline of manners, and of very great moral and national corruption; and its extraordinary success must be partly explained by the prevalence of a sort of intellectual and moral disease, which had overpowered the spirits of men after the fall of the ancient civilization and under the demoralizing influence of the gradual collapse of the great Roman empire. But even at that time those who stood intellectually high and looked deeply to things recognized the whole danger of this new turn of mind, and it is very remarkable that the best and most benevolent of the Roman emperors, such as Marcus Aurelius, Julian, etc., were the most zealous persecutors of Christianity, whilst it was tolerated by the bad ones, such as Commodus, Heliogabalus, etc. When it had gradually attained the superiority, one of its first sins against intellectual progress consisted in the destruction by Christian fanaticism of the calibrated Library of Alexandria, which contained all the intellectual treasures of antiquity—an incalculable loss to science, which can never be replaced. It is usually asserted in praise of Christianity that in the middle ages the Christian monasteries were the preservers of science and literature, but even this is correct only in a very limited sense, since boundless ignorance and rudeness generally prevailed in the monasteries, and innumerable ecclesiasts could not even read. Valuable literary treasures on parchment contained in the libraries of the monasteries were destroyed, the monks when they wanted money selling the books as parchment, or tearing out the leaves and writing psalms upon them. Frequently they entirely effaced the ancient classics, to make room for their foolish legends and homilies; nay, the reading of the classics, such as Aristotle for example, was directly forbidden by papal decrees.

"In New Spain Christian fanaticism immediately destroyed whatever of arts and civilization existed among the natives, and that this was not inconsiderable is shown by the numerous monuments now in ruins which place beyond a doubt the former existence of a tolerably high degree of culture. But in the place of this not a trace of Christian civilization is now to be observed among the existing Indians, and the resident Catholic clergy keep the Indians purposely in a state of the greatest ignorance and stupidity (see, Richthofen, Die Zustande der Republic Mexico, Berlin, 1854).

"Thus Christianity has always acted consistently in accordance with the principles of one of the fathers of the Church, Tertullian, who says: 'Desire of knowledge is no longer necessary since Jesus Christ, nor is investigation necessary since the Gospel.' If the civilization of the European and especially of Christian Nations has notwithstanding made such enormous progress in the course of centuries, an unprejudiced consideration of history can only tell us that this has taken place not by means of Christianity, but in spite of it. And this is a sufficient indication to what an extent this civilization must still be capable of development when once it shall be completely freed from the narrow bounds of old superstitious and religious embarrassments!"

"We must therefore endeavor to form convictions which are not to stand once and for all, as philosophers and theologians usually do, but such as may change and become improved with. the advance of knowledge. Whoever does not recognize this and gives himself up once for all to a belief which he regards as final truth, whether it be of a theological or philosophical kind, is of course incapable of accepting a conviction supported upon scientific grounds. Unfortunately our whole education is founded upon an early systematic curbing and fettering of the intellect in the direction of dogmatic (philosophical or theological) doctrines of faith, and only a comparatively small number of strong minds succeed in after years in freeing themselves by their own powers from these fetters, whilst the majority remain captive in the accustomed bonds and form their judgment in accordance with the celebrated saying of Bishop Berkeley: 'Few men think; but all will have opinions.'"— Buchner, Man in the Past, Present, and Future."